Praise for *Leading on the Frontline*

The book is a compelling read for those who have a genuine desire to be the best leader, whether a CEO with oversight for thousands of employees or a young business student starting out on their professional journey. It is also a truly gripping and memorable collection of Linda's adventures on the frontline. I hope you find the book and the story of Linda's life as enlightening, inspirational and transformational as I have.

Alan Hassenfeld, Director, Hasbro Inc., USA

I've been privileged to witness Linda's ability to inspire, motivate and galvanise a group of individuals into a formidable and determined team, ready to face anything together. In this book, Linda tells several remarkable, true stories of leadership where the stakes can't get much higher and the lessons land with real impact. She not only shows you what real leadership looks like, she makes you want to be a better person too. If Indiana Jones wanted to become a better business leader, he'd start by reading this book.

Bryan Adams, CEO and Founder, Ph.Creative, UK

Linda Cruse is an unstoppable force of nature who has much to teach us about empathy and leadership through her selfless (and sometimes quite terrifying) adventures on the frontline. I have had the honour of being on a 'Be The Change' trip, out of my comfort zone, where she led, inspired and enabled us to use our business brains to provide a hand-up for the local community—an experience which certainly changed me.

Karen Emanuel, CEO, Key Production (London) Ltd, UK

Great leaders shine during times of hardship and struggle. Linda is uniquely qualified to help share the wisdom of leadership as she has been on the frontlines with leaders during some of the most trying times imaginable. She has witnessed examples of extraordinary courage and also witnessed leadership failures, all captured through engaging storytelling in her new book. Her positive spirit, compassionate heart, global experience and crystal clear focus on what's important make this book a must read for leaders everywhere.

Jean Oelwang, President and Trustee, Virgin Unite

If you genuinely want to develop into an incredible leader or are running an organisation and struggle to find ways to engage with your staff or make a meaningful contribution—then this book, *Leading on the Frontline*, is a must-read.

Lawrence Wosskow, CEO, Wilson LLC, USA

One of the most rewarding experiences of my professional career was participating as a mentor in a recent 'Race4Good'. While our team's primary goal was to help families in need, it was these very families that gave us the invaluable lessons learned through enduring hardship, valuing community and teamwork that will last a lifetime. In Linda's latest book, *Leading on the Frontline,* her values, principles and desire to make a difference in the world, are distilled in what I would refer to as a business and life manual.

Charles L. Black III, Managing Director of Luxury, Compass, USA

Leading on the Frontline is a monument to courage and the capacity for each of us to change lives and our future for the better. It is a must-read for those with a passion to live a life of meaning, significance and impact at a time when we need it most.

Simon Mainwaring, CEO of We First and New York Times bestselling author, USA

Redmaids' High School alumna, Linda Cruse, perfectly embodies our school values and ethos. We need more global citizens with her drive, commitment and knowledge if we are to tackle international challenges relating to health, education and poverty. We are delighted she is working closely with us, running highly-educational, overseas humanitarian trips for our students. Together, we aim to develop the leaders of the future.

Isabel Tobias, Headmistress, Redmaids' High School, UK

Linda Cruse is a breath of fresh air—make that a force of nature! I have never met anyone with her force, drive and can-do approach to the most challenging of humanitarian and leadership situations. Her infectious personality positively carries you along and you cannot help but be inspired by her drive to make and Be The Change.

Jon Brown, Virgin Limited Edition, UK

A captivating and compelling read. Linda shares the powerful leadership lessons she has learnt through her unfathomable experiences as a humanitarian aid worker on the frontline.

Kim Ross, Collaboration Designer for Social Impact, Australia

No amount of pre reading or learning can quite prepare you for the frontline. Taking part in my own 'Be The Change' experience in Nepal, I was ready to fully embrace anything that came my way. Linda's passion, leadership and clear direction meant as a team we could successfully execute our mission to help the most vulnerable through an economic hand-up. I left Nepal with not only a lifetime of memories but a sense of purpose, fulfilment and gratitude. An experience not to be missed!

Elsa Renton, GlaxoSmithKline, New Zealand

Linda is the real deal! She is overflowing with all the 'good stuff': passion, purpose, positivity, productivity, and persistence. Linda is an amazing light in this world that is spreading compassion, hope and love for humanity everywhere she goes. I have been in emergency response and disaster management for 23 years, with my most recent (and still ongoing) being the recovery and rebuilding efforts in the BVI in the aftermaths of Hurricanes Irma and Maria. Linda has been a breath of fresh air in a time and space that has been stifling and overwhelming, and she has helped to rekindle my passion and renew my faith in humanity as well as polished the tarnish off my purpose. This book is a must read for everyone from 9 to 99, from the 'poorest' man to the 'richest' man, and from the man sitting in the corner office at the corporate headquarters to the man sitting on the corner of the street. They say that another man's experience is indeed the best teacher—Linda provides an immense and equally useful trove of 'nuggets' that we can all benefit from and share with others. This is not fiction, this is not fluffed—this is real. Anything realer than this is to be beside her on the frontline.

Dwayne J. Strawn, CEO, D. J. Strawn & Associates,
British Virgin Islands

This book will be useful to those who tread the unknown in this uncertain world. Linda, who I know well, has made a career in encouraging and developing leadership in difficult circumstances. As a retired solider and having served in Bosnia and Northern Ireland, I appreciate perhaps more than most what it takes to keep a cool head in difficult and dangerous situations. For those who may face such problems in the future, this book will help.

Major General Sir Evelyn Webb-Carter,
British Army Officer (Retd), UK

Linda's intensely personal stories will inspire you to examine your own life. Through this absolutely unique and amazing book, you will discover lessons about empathy, courage, surrender, compassion, leadership and other traits that are essential to being fully human and fully alive. I highly recommend this book for anyone who seeks to make a positive difference in the world.

Joseph Kerski, Education Manager, Esri, USA

It has been my pleasure to be part of Linda's journey which I would call 'how life should be lived'. Not many people have Linda's courage and zeal and as a business leader I admire the unique way she tackles human crises through leadership and entrepreneurship. I am sure Linda's book will provide a new dimension to business leaders to create a balance between their work life and giving back.

Mujeebullah Khan, CEO, iTextiles, Pakistan

Linda Cruse's *Leading on the Frontline* is the next step in breaking out of the old hierarchic mindset that stunts creativity and causes the downfall of companies that can't adapt as technology and culture change faster than anyone ever thought possible. Although not a textbook about technology or even change, the leadership lessons from this book allow us to create organizations that are adaptable to any kind of new situation, organizations that thrive and grow through times of failure, organizations that are full of people eager to come to work every day to fulfil the mission of the company.

Lise Laurin, CEO, EarthShift Global, USA

Leading on the Frontline captures Linda Cruse's exhilarating adventures from the front line of global disasters. Linda is a truly inspiring international humanitarian aid worker and demonstrates how courage, passion, selflessness and determination can transform you into a great leader.

Kerry-Ann dos Santos, Ironman and Ultra runner,
British Virgin Islands

Through her writing, Linda showcases her alchemical talents and gives us the ingredients necessary to develop world-class leadership skills. Her stories from the frontline inspire us to think differently. We learn that it's not about us; rather, it's about us serving something bigger than ourselves. A few words of caution: as you read this book, your soul – inevitably – will come calling!

Rita Ciolek, CPA, MFA, Filmmaker, USA

Linda Cruse is the epitome of someone who leads from the front. But, like the best (but by no means all) leaders, that's not about ego, it's about what achieves the best results. On the frontline of humanitarian crises all over the world Linda has inspired people to rebuild their lives and rediscover their self-respect.

David Lascelles, Earl of Harewood, UK

Having attended Linda's workshops over the years, she demonstrates how telling stories is a great way to engage people. However, telling real stories that enable you to apply her lessons learnt to your business leadership style is not just engaging, it's powerful.

Mark Dolan, Consultant, Sysdoc, New Zealand

I found I was holding my breath while reading about Linda's harrowing events that in the end have helped many souls. As an educator, I see the many lessons we can take from her work. Ironically, more developed societies can learn from the developing world on how to function better, in terms of human relations, priority setting and holistic views.

Dr Kelly Edmonds, E-Learning Specialist, Canada

Linda's book changes the way you look at life and your ability to overcome real and imaginary obstacles that stop us from excelling as extraordinary leaders. Linda is the real deal! I have travelled with Linda on 'Be The Change' trips and 'Race4Good' challenges. Reading about her courageous life's work is an inspiring window into what's possible for all of us.

Lesley Smith, Motivational Speaker and Change Maker,
Lesley Smith Productions, USA

Linda's work as a humanitarian has given her a unique insight into some of the purest elements of leadership. How does one lead when lives are at stake? Can one taken lessons from leadership on those edges and apply them to our more fortunate challenges in the developed world? Through her story, Linda gives the reader a chance to reflect on these questions, and much more.

Dolly Singh, Founder and CEO, Thesis Couture, USA

Recently we drew on Linda's ingenious program, Race4Good, to help us find ways to tackle the serious issue of food insecurity in Vail Valley. Led by Linda, the Race proved to be beyond our dreams—who would have thought that in just four hours disparate teams could produce such meaningful and insightful business plans. Linda loves her work and we loved playing with her huge heart!

Kat Haber, Curator, TEDxVail, USA

Linda Cruse is an exceptionally capable humanitarian and leader as well as a terrific writer—able to draw the reader in so we feel we are with her on her amazing adventures. I loved her first book, *Marmalade and Machine Guns*, and now she's written another winner. Get ready for a terrific read and to be inspired and motivated to make the world a better place.

Claire Fordham, Writer and Producer, USA

Being a single mother and an entrepreneur takes courage, curiosity, resilience and passion. So many people think that working for oneself is the easier way out than being an employee. This story reflects what many female entrepreneurs endure, juggling and multitasking, with little thanks for many years. I am so proud to know Linda who is telling a story so many of us want to tell.

Seonaid Mackenzie, Managing Partner, Sturgeon Ventures LLP, UK

Without individuals like Linda, the vast needs of the developing world's poorest and neediest would continue to be under-addressed. It is amazing what leadership she has demonstrated without the support of traditional institutional backing. Through her continued conviction to help others in need, Linda has inspired many to recognize how they can make a difference in the world in their own way.

Heather Potters, Chief Business Development Officer,
Vice-Chairman, Co-Founder, PharmaJet Inc., USA

Linda understands the need to maintain a level of compassion in the face of adversity. Her ability to hear those around her—no matter the class or culture—is a testament of true leadership. This book empowers leaders to think outside the box while staying grounded in the humanity around them.

Michelle Mercier, CEO, Create Honesty, USA

Linda Cruse is one of the most inspirational, courageous and genuine leaders I've ever met. Linda leads by example; her enthusiasm and passion for her work inspires others to get out of their comfort zone and join her on one of her humanitarian adventures. Linda combines her passion for humanitarian aid work with practical entrepreneurial solutions in the spirit of her 'hand-up not a hand-out' approach to aid work. I was introduced to Linda by the former British Consul General of Los Angeles as I was looking to give something back to the world; I wanted to use the skills I had learnt during my career in business to help those in need, meeting Linda was meant to be.

David Freeman, International Corporate Banker, USA

I first heard Linda talk at a networking event and was immediately inspired by her story of working on the frontline of disasters worldwide. In this book Linda shares personal life lessons of courage, trust, empathy, resilience, innovation, passion and more—a rich tapestry of what it takes to lead under the direst of circumstances. I commend Linda's story to anyone looking for inspiration. From the lessons shared here those of us in business can find much that is relevant to our own experience and be inspired to lift our own leadership to a new level with courage and passion.

Karen Fistonich, Chair, Villa Maria Wine Estates, New Zealand

There are not many people in the world who would be prepared to give up their comfortable and secure lives and travel to the frontline of human suffering, on their own with little support network in place. Linda is one of those special people. I have had the pleasure of knowing Linda for some time and to watch with admiration as she continues to work her magic in places where help is needed. *Leading on the Frontline* is a topic Linda knows well and her book will take a special place in my collection of must-reads.

**Chris Hawker, Director, Emergency Management Otago,
New Zealand**

A mixture of high-octane energy and high-octave notes remove any doubt as to who is to be followed when solutions are required. Linda Cruse has the gift to lead and that gift is not squandered on ego; it is lavished on the less fortunate. Her drive, courage and decency has been tested beyond most limits and her stoic resolve is inspirational. Linda is a true friend of humanity.

Ivor Wood, Director, Pathway Risk Management, UK

Linda's work is that of a true warrior. By comparing her work in the frontline with that of business leaders, she is making it real and worthy of the best of human endeavours, something that is easily forgotten in the business world. Through this book and through her leadership programmes, she is applying the best of her leadership to uncover solutions for the wellbeing of many.

**Salvador Acevedo, Vice President of Culture Strategy,
Scansion Inc., USA**

Linda is the embodiment of humanity at its best; an incredible leader, dedicated to saving life and providing uplift for forgotten communities. She is a hero who leads where help is needed the most, sometimes regardless of her own safety. This book captures the extraordinary narrative that is Linda's life and contains invaluable lessons for today's business leaders.

Nelofar Currimbhoy, President, Shahnaz Herbals, India

Linda has travelled the globe and learned hard lessons along the way that now make her the most phenomenal teacher. If you want to learn about leadership, then find a comfy chair, pick up this book and be inspired by Linda. In my opinion, if you do not read this book, you are totally missing out##...##on adventure, on learning, on life. Don't let life pass you by like that. Grab it! Now!

Helen Jamieson, Managing Director, Jaluch Ltd, UK

Working with Linda was nothing short of a life-changing experience. While years of experience can sometimes turn professionals into rigid traditionalists, Linda's decades in the field have only increased her creativity. She's mastered her tools, allowing her to approach any situation with flexibility and clarity and understanding that no two cases can be treated exactly the same. As a young person with high ambitions, Linda showed me that the concept of leaders-as-saviours is flawed, that true leaders unlock the potential in the people around them. Linda helped me find and use my strengths to create genuine positive change in the world. She will do the same for you.

Dan Patel, University of California, USA

Linda Cruse is someone who walks her talk, a woman of ACTION. Her frontline work is real, on the ground, tough and dirty and provides lasting impact in communities. The tacit knowledge she has about what works and what doesn't is captured in focused leadership lessons that will resonate with today's business leaders and university students.

Manisha Javeri, Associate Professor, California State University, USA

Linda imparts important leadership wisdom. Among them, that it's not about you and that in a life of leadership, your list of teachers is usually longer than your list of accomplishments. Her book shows the way to be your best self on your own frontline. I met Linda on my own frontline: working with students to change paradigms and change realities, and I recommend you meet her on your own frontline, by reading this book.

**Rachel Christensen, Center for Peace and Commerce,
University of San Diego, USA**

Linda's book is filled with stories of courage and perseverance on the frontline that will leave you ready to book a flight! Taking part in a recent 'Race4Good' was an opportunity of a lifetime. Being able to provide a village with an economic hand-up by working with a wide range of professionals pushed me to discover my true passions, hone my business leadership skills and encouraged me to stretch myself further than I ever thought possible. From courage to empathy to communication, Linda shows us how to be the best leaders through a unique frontline humanitarian lens.

Veerali Juthani, Student, University of Southern California, USA

As a student of Claremont McKenna College, I worked directly with Linda Cruse and became captivated by her mindset and philosophy of leadership. Linda has shown me that leadership is a method of understanding and responding to people and situations and begins with an internal evaluation of yourself. This is how change can occur and real-world humanitarian problems can be solved, whether in the university, at work, or on the frontline.

Hunter Kettering, Claremont McKenna College, USA

Through compelling storytelling, *Leading on the Frontline* not only entertains with suspenseful accounts from remote corners of the world but enriches with knowledge on how to improve your approach to life. No matter who you are or who you want to be, Linda's stories and shared wisdom will empower you to become a better person, and consequently a better leader. It is an exquisite collection of powerful experiences that you'll find difficult to put down and will want to read again and again.

Cinzia Angelini, Animation Filmmaker, USA

Linda's mission is to transform, and I can confirm that her influence is nothing short of transformative. Her unique angle on development facilitates a symbiotic experience — enhancing the livelihoods of the individuals in the communities she works with as well as those of the business leaders and students she takes to the frontline.

**Khadija Hassanali, former Student,
Claremont McKenna College, USA**

Inspirational, enlightening, and universally applicable, *Leading on the Frontline* is imperative for students who crave leadership advice beyond the classroom. Taking a unique storytelling approach, this book propels you into the complexities of the frontline where you must rise to the challenge. The transformative lessons I received as a member of a 'Race4Good' team in Nepal are seamlessly incorporated into her narrative so that everyone can benefit from her innovative strategies to living a life of meaning.

Alexa Libro, Student, University of California, Los Angeles, USA

LEADING

ON THE

FRONTLINE

LEADING

ON THE

FRONTLINE

REMARKABLE STORIES AND
ESSENTIAL LEADERSHIP LESSONS FROM
THE WORLD'S DANGER ZONES

LINDA CRUSE

WILEY

First published in 2019 by John Wiley & Sons Australia, Ltd
42 McDougall St, Milton Qld 4064

Office also in Melbourne

Typeset in 11.5/15pt Bembo Std Regular

© John Wiley & Sons Australia, Ltd 2019

The moral rights of the author have been asserted

A catalogue record for this book is available from the National Library of Australia

Cover design: Wiley

Cover Image: © Jose A. Bernat Bacete/Getty Images

Cover and internal photos: Linda Cruse

Printed in Singapore by C.O.S. Printers Pte Ltd

10 9 8 7 6 5 4 3 2 1

Disclaimer
The material in this publication is of the nature of general comment only, and does not represent professional advice. It is not intended to provide specific guidance for particular circumstances and it should not be relied on as the basis for any decision to take action or not take action on any matter which it covers. Readers should obtain professional advice where appropriate, before making any such decision. To the maximum extent permitted by law, the author and publisher disclaim all responsibility and liability to any person, arising directly or indirectly from any person taking or not taking action based on the information in this publication.

To Stan and Doreen Cruse, my wonderful mum and dad,
who gave me the courage, confidence and sense of adventure
to follow my passion and purpose,
and who daily fill our lives with love, fun and magic!
Thank you!

Go to the people.
Live with them.
Learn from them.
Start with what they know.
Build with what they have.
But with the best leaders,
When the work is done,
The task accomplished,
The people will say,
We have done this ourselves!

Lao Tzu

Contents

Foreword by
Sir Richard Branson

I first heard about Linda Cruse through her fearless, compassionate and practical approach to humanitarian work in Thailand. Finding herself in the middle of chaotic scenes, Linda pulled together a high-level taskforce to provide a business 'hand-up' for hundreds of survivors of the Asian tsunami. From this moment, her reputation as a courageous humanitarian leader had been established and I wondered how I could involve her in the work of my foundation, Virgin Unite. Soon after, Linda and I worked together for the first time, it was 2005 and we were in Soweto, South Africa leading a group of international business leaders, demonstrating how business can be a 'force for good'. Linda, in her usual yes-style approach to my request, had flown over to assist.

Three years later, we're in Morocco. A failed hot air balloon experiment in the late 1990s had led me to Marrakech, where I had fallen in love with the Moroccan people and their country. I wanted to do something that would support them and bring more people to this beautiful place, so with the encouragement of my parents, I bought a crumbling citadel and set about transforming it into the Kasbah Tamadot hotel. Prior to opening, we worked hard to train members of the Berber community to take on the roles of head of departments, waiters, cooks, housekeepers and receptionists. It wasn't easy, but we did it. Following the official opening, I began to look beyond the walls of the hotel for ways to uplift the surrounding community and asked Linda to come to Morocco to help.

Linda didn't hesitate, having traded all her worldly possessions for a suitcase nearly two decades earlier, she was always ready to go wherever she was needed. For the next 18 months, Linda lived among the local Berbers, leading major projects on behalf of Virgin Unite. Whilst immersed in the community, she discovered a local association growing herbs, spices and other produce and immediately recognised a business opportunity which could dramatically uplift the wider community. It was her astute eye, quick thinking and resourcefulness which led the local Berber farmers to create a successful cooperative growing the most expensive spice on the planet—saffron. It was the start of a wonderful relationship. Tamadot guests jumped at the chance to visit local projects, to meet the Berber community and buy direct from artisans and our head chef began purchasing as much saffron as he could. Thanks to Linda's entrepreneurial eye, honey, olive oil, spices, herbs and saffron all found their way into the hotel's kitchen. Since then, Linda has been a friend and advisor on countless Virgin Unite initiatives.

During her extraordinary career on the frontline, Linda has led projects for HRH The Prince of Wales, The Dalai Lama and countless international businesses. But name-dropping does not interest her! I have never met a more dedicated, committed and passionate humanitarian and courageous leader. What drives Linda is finding ways to uplift forgotten communities devastated by disaster, often in the world's greatest danger zones. She literally dives in where others fear to go. Heading to Thailand after the tsunami, to Pakistan after the earthquake, working in the Philippines following the typhoon and later in Nepal. Most recently, she was with me in the British Virgin Islands, working to create sustainable incomes for the hundreds of people whose homes and livelihoods have been devastated by Hurricane Irma. When thousands of people are fleeing the scene of a disaster, you find Linda flying in!

While working in these pressured, emotionally-charged, often chaotic environments, Linda keeps a cool head and instinctively looks around for opportunities for sustainable economic uplift. She is enormously compassionate, but her focus is always on achieving successful and measurable outcomes. She has the natural ability to identify potential in the most desperate situations, which is why I often say, 'Linda makes the impossible, possible'.

What I've witnessed is that she is a real person of action, willing to throw herself into a problem to solve it. You can count on Linda to deliver, always.

Her courage, determination and brilliant mind compel everyone around her to jump in, roll up their sleeves and put their all into making things happen—often resulting in creative, highly effective solutions that might never occur without her. She's a woman of action, who works at a fast pace to get things done and to create immediate impact.

As you'll find out in this book, Linda takes a real business approach to creating change. It's never just about the money. Linda learned early on that accepting a cheque will not solve a problem for long; the gold lies in getting the best and brightest brains to solve the biggest challenges. Above all, Linda is always tremendous fun! I think that's a big part of how she gets so much done.

Linda's book presents a powerful new perspective on what it means to truly lead. It captures her extraordinary leadership abilities and illustrates how one person can make a difference. Combined with Linda's compelling adventures and misadventures, *Leading on the Frontline* provides invaluable insights for today's business leaders and is a must-read for anyone who has a genuine desire to be the best leader they can be.

Lastly, while Linda happens to share my love of magic, I know that her ability to transform lives is one hundred percent real.

Sir Richard Branson

Acknowledgements

Huge thanks to those men and women with vision, too many to mention individually, who have supported and encouraged me on along the way, who include: Sir Richard Branson, HRH the Prince of Wales, Wanda Whitely, Mary Mills-Brown, Penny Godfrey, Robert Tunmore, Jacqui Smith, David Smith, Cathy Boutin, Lesley Smith, Beth Shafer, Jane Donaldson, Fadzai Marange, Rita Ciolek, Jon Craton, Mark Abramczyk, Karen Emanuel, Mujeeb Khan, Anna Stove, Alan Hassenfeld, Charles Black, Sue Hale and Julian Venables.

Appreciation and admiration to the numerous companies that I have worked alongside over the years, that have shared their gifts, their innovation, wisdom, creativity, intelligence and critical analysis for the empowerment of challenged communities worldwide, including Manpower, Cadbury's, Virgin, Hasbro, Nestlé, KPMG, Thai Beverage, Deloitte, Diageo, Accenture, Standard Chartered, Shahnaz Herbals, GSK, Hilton Hyland, Jo Malone, HSBC, Cross Colors, SpaceX, Wanda Group and many more.

Lastly, huge thanks to my wonderful family: Mum and Dad, who instilled in me my sense of wonder and adventure and who gave me the confidence to follow my heart and passion, and through all my craziness have cheered me on along the way. To my children and grandchildren: Gail, Gareth, Isla Rose, Luca and Theo, Graham, Michaela, Alfie, Teddy and Florence, each and every one of whom I carry in my heart as I climb the mountain, face the fear and celebrate the achievements. They cheer me on, teach me daily the true magic of life, and fill my soul with happiness, gratitude, love and laughter.

Some names and places in this book have been changed to respect the individuals' privacy and guard their personal safety. I wish, in so many cases, that I had been able to name them and honour the sterling work they are doing in such difficult circumstances. To these unsung heroes: thank you.

A note from the author:
How it all began

I had always heard that a near-death experience can change your life.
It's true.

I was getting by, making a living as a single mum. People told me I
should be proud of myself. By the last day of our annual sales conference
I just felt wired. Sell, sell, sell. I was worn out and desperate to get
home, to pull the duvet over my head and sleep forever. I decided to
drive home that night, as I often did, to avoid traffic. Luckily, the road
was almost empty.

One second I was driving along, struggling to stay awake, the next I was
blind. A moment of stabbing pain behind my eyes, then everything went
black. I don't know how I managed to pull onto the hard shoulder—
instinct, I suppose. Anyway, there I sat, whimpering in fear. Praying to a
God to whom I hadn't given a thought in decades.

My sight returned a few hours later. But in that dark time something
in me changed. It wasn't a nice feeling. It was disturbing, even
frightening. What I saw in those hours of blindness was that the life I
had been living was stifling me.

I had become a single mother in my early twenties and that,
understandably, had reduced my scope for adventure. I adored raising
my two children, but the free-spirited life of wide horizons that I later
found so exhilarating simply wasn't open to me. So I did what mothers
in my situation do: I got on with the job, my own needs well and truly
buried. I watched my two wonderful children grow and I got in the
groceries, paid the bills, raced to pick them up from school. Rushed

headlong through each day. Much of what I had was good. But I was in a meaningless job, selling something I didn't believe in, eating the wrong foods, drinking too much and crying under my duvet at night.

When a friend asked me what I wanted for my birthday, I asked for a blue suitcase. For three years it sat in the corner of my bedroom, where I could see it. I tacked photos from travel magazines on a cork board on my wall, and marked out my route with pins on a big map of the world. I dreamed and I planned. I put a little money away each month. And although I had to keep working for another three years, I was much happier. I had something to aim for. I didn't know anyone in the field of international aid work, but that wasn't going to stop me.

Then the right time came. It was the year my son left home to join the army and his older sister went to university. They were happily following their dreams. My job was done. One summer's evening after supper I looked at my darling children, all grown up, and said, 'Is it okay if I leave home?'

We laughed together, nestled up close on the sofa. 'Go, Mum! We are right behind you.'

Preface

I'm often asked, why do I do what I do? What drives me constantly to risk my life in disaster and conflict areas? Some people admire me; others think I'm crazy.

For as long as I can remember I have felt like I was on a 'mission'. From a very young age I was driven by an unquenchable thirst to serve something greater than myself, but for a long time I didn't know what, where or how.

My journey as a humanitarian aid worker has not been short of adventure, or misadventure. I have lost a few lives, escaped from a rebel army, narrowly evaded rape, been wrongfully arrested, been held at gunpoint, survived severe altitude sickness and hypothermia. Once I had my face slashed open, and in the absence of medical help had to stitch myself up. Very often I have little or no access to clean running water, reliable electricity, a dependable food supply, a comfy bed, hot showers or safe shelter. All of these things I once took for granted. I don't now.

The dangers faced by humanitarian aid workers continue to increase. For example, a shocking 30 per cent of aid workers are now deemed to be undercover spies. Governments are hungry to get closer to their 'targets' by whatever means, and who gets closest to the heart of these vulnerable communities? We do.

Once, when offered the protection of a heavily armoured 4x4 to travel into the tribal areas of Pakistan, my reflex response was, 'Do you really want me to die? If I travel in that, it would be like having an arrow pointing at my head labelled "I am important. Kill me".' I knew I was more likely to reach my village safely riding in a battered old taxi and wearing a shapeless *burkha*. This is how we live.

I have also learned the meaning of unconditional love, strength, forgiveness, courage and compassion from unconventional teachers. An 11-year-old tsunami survivor who lost not only her parents and siblings, but also her teacher, her home and most of her friends; a 16-year-old Burmese refugee blown up by a landmine, left blind and without legs, surviving in a border camp, unwelcome in his host country yet unable to return to his own — my list of teachers is long.

My first-hand experiences of fear, suffering and living life on the edge have given me unique insights into life and its meaning, and into leadership. Along the way I have also absorbed the wisdom of indigenous elders, Amazonian shamans, Tibetan lamas and Indian gurus, as well as visionaries as diverse as HH the Dalai Lama, HRH the Prince of Wales and Sir Richard Branson. But life itself has been my greatest teacher. My most important leadership skills have been gained, not from books or in classrooms, but from living and working for nearly two decades on the global disaster frontline.

The stories you'll discover here invite you into a world in which you may find few recognisable points of reference. I hope, by exposing you to this unfamiliar world, to give you the opportunity to learn about yourself and your potential impact on others. Engaging with these stories will test and expand your ability to develop emotionally engaged and purpose-driven leadership practices and build remarkable teams.

Through my 'Be The Change' leadership program I regularly lead teams of successful, highly individualistic business leaders and entrepreneurs to the frontline. Over and over I have observed how, once they are way outside their comfort zone, they discover untapped capabilities, strengths and vulnerabilities, and are in some way transformed by the experience. In this book I want to challenge your mindset. If, by the time you've finished, I have not transformed you in some way, I would be disappointed in myself.

Business leaders today face unparalleled change and uncertainty. Who is better equipped to meet the challenges of our volatile, uncertain, complex and ambiguous world than a frontline humanitarian? Leading on the frontline, you're trained to expect the unexpected, to be courageous in a crisis, capable of working with change, innovative, resilient, confident, compassionately present and engaged.

'*It's not about you.*' So my nursing matron taught me, at age 18, and that confronting admonition has inspired perhaps my best insights and results as a leader. An effective leader *enables*, harnessing and herding the power, energy and brilliance of the team by asking great questions and letting them work out the way forward. Deep empathy and emotional understanding are the foundation of a great leader.

The idea of writing *Leading on the Frontline* was kickstarted 18 months ago by a request from a large corporate who believe their current leadership programs are not delivering and that by sharing leadership insights from the frontline, I could inspire transformative emotional engagement.

I believe both my leadership program and the stories from the field collected in this book demonstrate convincingly that the frontline humanitarian model offers valuable insights for business leaders. The qualities and skills required to succeed in a complex frontline field operation are much the same as those needed in business. Composure under pressure, people and leadership skills, teamwork, perseverance and mental toughness are needed in both arenas.

Whether on the frontline or in the boardroom, envisioning the future, setting your strategic purpose, team alignment, values and culture, or customer service and focus, your objective will be not only to achieve the goals you have set but to exceed your expectations. To bring this symmetry into sharper focus here, in the 'leadership lessons' at the end of each story I have distilled my insights from the frontline experience and posed a few challenging questions that I hope will motivate you to reappraise your own professional strategies.

We can all learn from the extraordinary ways vulnerable people confront fear, face loss and find joy in the most dire circumstances. Through these stories I want to inspire you to get passionate about living, to embrace your courage, compassion and intuition, and to unearth the very best version of yourself so you can 'be all you can be' on your own frontline.

Part I

Courage

Courage is the first of human virtues because
it makes all others possible.

Aristotle

Have you missed out on
opportunities because you
failed to act quickly enough?

1

Courage

How an unexpected brush with the Nepali
police tapped into hidden depths of courage

In 1953, Edmund Hillary and his Sherpa companion Tenzing Norgay
pitched their tent beneath the summit of Mount Everest, at 27 900 feet.
On the morning of the final climb, Hillary emerged from the tent
to find his boots had frozen solid. After two hours spent thawing the
boots, the pair set out for the summit with 30-pound packs on their
backs. Faced with a 40-foot sheer rock face they remained undeterred
and, edging themselves along a crack in this great wall of rock, which
was later named the Hillary Step, they inched their way towards
the summit.

You only have to say 'Nepal' and people's eyes mist over with
romantic stories of courage and adventure. They think of brothers-
in-arms scaling the highest mountain on Earth. Or of Gurkha soldiers,
with their terrifying *kukri* blades, striking terror in the hearts of their
enemies. In more peaceful moments they might dream of Kathmandu,
a city immortalised in the songs of hippie bands. Love and peace.

Then other facts jostle for room. Hillary himself devoted the rest
of his life to raising funds to help the Sherpa people of the Himalayas.
This is revealing, as is the sheer number of young hopefuls seeking to
join the Gurkhas. As many as 28 000 try out for only 300 places each
year. As they vie desperately for selection, each of them has one goal

in mind: to get out of Nepal. Around 1600 Nepali men and women leave their homeland every day, bound for Malaysia, Qatar and other countries in the Middle East. The hard fact is that Nepal is one of the poorest countries on Earth, and money sent home from these migrant workers is often all that keeps their families from starvation.

There is no halo of love and peace over Kathmandu. Over the past 50 years political instability has brought the country to its knees. At the time I was working there, between 2001 and 2003, it was a dangerous place to be. Maoist rebels, operating mainly in rural areas, had stepped up their campaign of violence in a decade-long civil war in which they sought to end the monarchy and establish a people's republic. In November 2001, King Gyanendra imposed a State of Emergency and ordered his army to crush the rebels. For the next two years it was all-out war.

In what I now see as a delicious irony, I first came to Kathmandu in 2001 for a rest cure. I needed to get away from the chaos of India for a while. My doctor had suggested a break after I had fainted at the Delhi airport, suffering from burnout. There were two Tibetan refugee camps in Nepal, and the Tibet Relief Fund were happy for me to visit them and add to their body of research. Although Kathmandu clearly did not spell love and peace in these war-torn days, there was still something special about the place and I decided to stay on for a while.

When I arrived the war was showing no signs of ending. But in the city, apart from the enforced shoot-to-kill curfews, life carried on. And nothing stopped my frontline humanitarian work, especially as I had a great local team who had their ears to the ground to alert us if a big offensive was brewing.

Thamel, in the heart of the city, was a mecca for backpackers, trekkers and mountaineers of every nationality who headed there to shop and have fun. Shops and stalls selling Buddhist statues and shawls, puppets and paper lanterns shared space with trekking stores. Tourists happily picked their way through this shoppers' paradise of hippie souvenirs and the latest North Face climbing and camping equipment. In the evenings, on street corners and in crowded nightclubs, bands played seventies classic rock covers until the small hours.

It was at a nightclub that I first met Karma. He approached me, no doubt intrigued by seeing a Western woman in the crowd of jostling partygoers. Tall and broad, with flat, almost Mongolian features, there was something so confident about him that when he asked me to join his group of friends I felt compelled to follow him. I was quickly to learn that Karma's confidence was matched by a warm-hearted desire to do good. As soon as he heard that I was involved in a charitable project he made sure I had all the help I needed. It turned out that he was one of a rare breed—a dependable free spirit. Over the years he was to become my fixer, requisition officer, PA and travel companion rolled into one.

Our friendship grew quickly, helped by the fact that Karma saved my life more than once. I could not have survived—and I certainly wouldn't have achieved very much—without Karma. His local knowledge and the respect others had for him were invaluable. Without him I would have come unstuck in the early days in Nepal. He took care of my health and safety, ensuring that my street food was well cooked and my utensils clean(ish). He tasted my drinks to check they weren't 'duplicate' (chemically spiked). On his motorbike he took me to places others rarely visited, negotiating treacherous mountain roads and helping me to find, meet and talk to the people we both wanted to help. Karma taught me to see and honour the invisible poor in Nepal, not the beggars and refugees but a whole exploited and downtrodden underclass. People such as the lowly guard who stood all night at a car park. Karma would always go out of his way to shake their hand, say a kind word, give them a coin. He was a master of random acts of kindness.

At first, Karma's friends were wary. When he brought me over to their table at the nightclub the night we met, they seemed uncomfortable. At one point, one of them took Karma aside and I could tell from the man's tense whispering and nervous glances that he was warning Karma not to associate with a Westerner. Karma explained to me later that in a country where the police and local government officials were invariably corrupt it was safest to keep your head down and not be noticed. A few weeks after our first meeting, something happened that helped me understand their point of view.

We were in the same nightclub at 11 on a Saturday night and the dance floor was heaving. Taking a break from dancing, we were drinking beer at a table near the bar when the music suddenly stopped and the lights were thrown on. For a moment, I felt like a teenager again, half expecting a teacher to step forward and read the riot act. Instead, six policemen barged through the swing doors of the club. Everyone stilled, rooted to the spot. Apart from the clatter of their heavy boots on the polished floor, the silence was absolute. The uniformed men stood in a line and shouted, brandishing heavy wooden sticks at us. I could feel the tension in the room. Not fear exactly but a kind of waiting, as if a breath had been taken and not yet expelled. There was anticipation, as if each person was waiting to see which one of them would be picked out. I sensed it had happened before and they knew the drill.

One of the policemen saw me and a handful of other foreigners. In broken English, he bellowed at us, 'Get out. Go! Go now!' Then, when some Nepalis started sidling to the door, he barked, 'All Nepalis stay.'

A group of tourists stampeded for the staircase. I didn't move. Alok, the youngest of our group, said to me, 'Go with the others!' I was furious. 'Why should I? They've no right…'

'They will get what they came for. Just go.'

When Karma saw that I was not getting up he pulled me to my feet and gently pushed me towards the door.

'Go,' he whispered. 'Please. There is nothing you can do.'

I started heading for the door then thought better of it. Instead, I walked up to the policeman who had been doing the shouting and stood facing him, eye to eye. He grabbed my arm and tried to push me in the direction of the door but I stood firm. His pungent body odour made me want to heave.

'I leave when they leave,' I said, fists clenched at my sides.

The more he shouted, the more I stood firm. By now, his colleagues had formed a circle around us, curious to see which one of us would break the standoff. The policeman looked away first. A moment later, with a quick motion to his men, they left.

Later, I sat with Karma and his friends at our regular roadside café, sharing a jug of beer.

'You're one crazy woman, Linda,' Karma said. I sipped my beer as the guys chatted animatedly in Hindi.

'What would they have done?' I asked Karma.

Without saying anything, Mingma, one of Karma's friends, bent to slip off his shoes and socks. He showed me the soles of his feet which were scarred with blackened puncture marks.

'First they tie our hands behind our backs,' Karma said. 'Then they put our ankles in...' He searched for the word.

'Stocks?' I suggested.

'Right. Then wood with nails in it. They beat us on our feet.'

'What do they want?' I asked.

'Money,' Alok said, giggling nervously. 'Money to buy tea!' Karma explained that if someone was not able to give even the smallest bribe, enough for a cup of tea, they would be beaten. No one complained. To do so was seen as a sign of weakness. Anyway, the police stuck together. If anyone spoke out, they would simply make up a worse charge. Better to tough it out. I blustered about the injustice of it all and Karma watched me, smiling.

'Welcome to Nepal, Linda.'

He raised his glass to me and his friends joined him in the toast. I sensed that I was now a full-fledged member of their company, and I couldn't help blushing with pleasure.

Leadership lesson #1

Courage means speaking out in support of the people we care about and the values we believe in. It means taking risks in order to do the right thing, even when the safer course might be to remain silent. True leaders are judged by their actions and example: it's what they do, not the position they hold, that makes them great. Stand up and be counted. Hope is not a plan.

***

Great leaders inspire with passion, and encourage and cheerlead their people when times are tough. They demonstrate courage and clarity when the hard decisions must be made.

- Where is courage required in your role?
- When do you feel you need to be more courageous?
- What do you need to put in place to ensure this?

Himalayas, Nepal

When was the last time you allowed someone else to make a major decision and let go of the outcome, with total trust?

2

Trust

How an encounter with a rebel unit in Nepal forced me to let go and trust

Three months after I arrived in Nepal, I set out with Karma to find a village in the east of the country, four hours north of a hill station named Hille. I had been tasked by one of the local NGOs with conducting a basic needs assessment as well as looking out for signs of human trafficking. The confusion of the civil war had led to an increase in the number of girls being drugged and kidnapped, and the NGO wanted to know the scale of the problem. Most girls, I had been told, were taken to Mumbai and forced to work in brothels. Some were as young as 12.

Karma had suggested it would be safer if we travelled in a group, but I thought he was being overcautious. Later I wished I had listened to him.

We had to pass through numerous checkpoints. Maoist rebels usually armed their pillion riders as they could more easily wield a gun with both arms free. As a result, at each checkpoint I had to dismount and join a queue for an arms inspection. As soon as the soldiers saw I was a foreigner they brought me to the front of the line, but it still slowed our progress.

On the road, Karma rode fast and confidently, honking his way past long lines of Tata trucks. Up front the cabs of the trucks were edged with fairy lights while at the back the all-seeing eye glared at us. As we overtook them the drivers would flick a switch and an array of trumpety horns on the roofs of their cabs would play a multitude of tunes. Although invariably drunk or buzzed on stimulant drinks to keep themselves awake, they were not half as dangerous as the drivers of the local minibuses, who drove at breakneck speed, overtaking three abreast on blind corners. Karma told me they were paid an attractive bonus calculated on the speed of their journey, so were prepared to risk their lives. Every now and again we passed the crumpled shells of vehicles that didn't make it.

Karma and I were on a trail bike, so it was relatively easy to take a break from the chaos of the main road. Whenever he could, he turned off the highway, escaping onto rough, stony roads chiselled out of the mountainside. It was not much safer on these mountain passes but it was a blessing to be free of the pollution and noise. We stopped frequently to answer the complaints of the troubled bike. Only a few army-controlled petrol pumps had clean, undoctored fuel. The rest, especially in the outlying areas, were invariably contaminated and clogged up the arteries of the engine. In a poor country like Nepal, people are used to fixing things with anything that comes to hand. Whatever can be welded, stapled, glued or nailed is repaired, however old or defunct. There was no shortage of mechanics to tend to Karma's bike and they would use a variety of makeshift tools. The funnel used to pour in the oil was a large rolled-up leaf and the humble wire coat hanger, twisted into all sorts of shapes, turned out to be a most effective multi-tool. But these were only ever temporary fixes and we always had to stop again after a couple of hours.

Because of the army roadblocks and repeated breakdowns, our journey took far longer than we anticipated. Given the 8 pm curfew, Karma decided we should stop at a friend's house for the night. It was a typical wooden farmer's home on stilts with the ground floor reserved for the animals, a simple but functional place with squat toilets across the yard. The men of the house greeted us with a warm *Namaste*, palms together and a nod of the head. The women hung back at first, their hands held up in front of their faces, giggling shyly.

We sat around a bonfire outside, eating dhal, vegetables and rice, while the men told stories. Later one of them played a guitar. In the firelight I could see the shadows of scars crisscrossing their faces. I noticed that one of the men was missing a finger, a calling card of the Maoists. At one point I heard the sound of what I took to be fireworks. I asked one of the men if the village was holding a festival and felt very foolish, and not a little apprehensive, when he replied that it was gunfire. A raid on the local police station had been predicted that night.

The chilly air finally drove us all indoors and we climbed the ladder to the first floor. Once we were all inside, the ladder was removed and the trap door bolted shut. I hoped I wouldn't need the toilet before morning. As was the custom, all eight of us lay down together on the floor, lined up in rows like sardines in a tin. I was the last to lie down and as I carefully picked my way across the sleeping bodies I noticed that each man was holding his *kukri*, unsheathed. I felt both fascinated and repelled. I had heard that in times past if a *kukri* was drawn in combat, it had to 'taste blood'. I hoped it was just a myth.

The next morning the old man of the group saw me watching him clean his *kukri*, which he did with great tenderness. He asked me if I would like a lesson. Before I could respond he leapt nimbly to his feet and started to demonstrate the moves. He showed me how you had to first slap the knife against the skin of your opponent, next turning the blade quickly with a flick of the wrist, then slicing firmly downwards. He gave me the knife and my arm buckled under the weight of it.

I remembered a story a British diplomat in Delhi once told me. An angry crowd had gathered in the streets of the city, preparing to riot. The police and paramilitary had arrived armed with rifles, but the crowd refused to budge. Things were getting nasty; it was a powder keg ready to explode. Then a unit of Gurkhas showed up with their *kukris* drawn. In seconds the protesters stopped what they were doing and walked away in silence. I could well believe it.

We left later that morning, each man embracing Karma firmly. They warned him to be careful and I sensed they were concerned that we were setting out on our own without backup. We travelled fast on the windy mountain track. The small villages we passed seemed oddly deserted. I had a distinct feeling we were being watched. I felt unnerved by the silence, my eyes searching constantly for signs of life. Occasionally, when we passed through a small settlement, I'd think I saw something moving in the shadows—a flash of colour perhaps—but otherwise the only signs of life were the birds of prey circling high above us, occasionally diving to spear a small creature for dinner.

By late afternoon I needed a break. I desperately wanted to stretch my legs.

'Can we stop?'

'Not here.'

'Please Karma,' I begged. 'My back is aching, and I need the toilet.'

We continued to bump our way along the rutted track. 'I have a bad feeling about this place,' Karma said. 'It's too quiet.'

Karma was usually so self-assured. Nothing ruffled him. I'd never seen him like this. I saw him glance at his fuel gauge, which showed just over a quarter of a tank. The wind had picked up and I moved my body a little closer to his. Soon we entered a densely forested area and the track became narrow and overgrown. At one point we swerved to avoid a hare and I gave a little yelp.

'Keep quiet, Linda!' I could feel the muscles in Karma's back, rigid with tension.

I was cursing the blithe and careless way I had laughed off Karma's fears. He had warned me it would be better to travel in a group. 'What if the bike breaks down?' he had said. 'How could I leave you alone if I had to get help?'

Karma took a corner too fast and we skidded on the damp undergrowth. We managed to steady ourselves and when we looked up Karma slammed on the breaks. A man blocked our path. We were looking straight into the barrel of a gun.

Karma shouted at me, 'Take your helmet off now!'

In a split second my blond hair was flying loose. The man with the gun froze, shocked to see a foreign woman. Then he shouted furiously at Karma. I knew him to be a Maoist by the red bandana he wore. We were in a lot of trouble. The rebel soldier jabbed me with the steel butt of his gun, forcing me to dismount. I was trembling, certain he would shoot me. As I stood whimpering, the gun barrel pointed at my chest, all I could think about was that it was my son's birthday the next day and he would wonder why I hadn't called.

Karma spoke then, his voice steady. 'Do as he says. No sudden moves.'

The man led us at rifle point to a clear piece of ground on a hillside, which was their camp. There were about forty young men and girls, painfully thin. Each one held a bamboo stick. They looked like kids who had bunked off school and didn't quite know what to do with themselves. For a moment I wanted to switch into head teacher mode and tell them off, but then I remembered the stories I had heard.

Only a week before, I had read of a 32-year-old subsistence farmer from western Nepal being singled out in a random night-time attack. Her attackers were also young. They had taken her out onto the porch where they bound her hands behind her back and tied her ankles together. Next, they put a large rock under her knee. One of them showed her an axe, then while several kids held her down, three others took turns hacking at her knees. There were pieces of flesh and bone all over the porch the next morning.

The Maoist rebels had conscripted large numbers of teenage boys and girls. Although their real enemy was the Royal Nepal Army, who were on the receiving end of some of the most horrific acts of torture, including slicing off soldiers' testicles or tying the young men to electric fires and watching them burn, ordinary Nepalis were also at risk. The rebels wanted to be heard, and acts of cruelty were a sickeningly effective way of getting attention.

I looked around the camp. The ground was heavily scarred, with large patches of burnt grass. The trees were split and blackened. All around us were torched vehicles, piles of broken bricks, and empty teargas and landmine shells. I wondered if this was where the rebels made their infamous pressure cooker bombs or the lethal homemade grenades they filled with bits of rusted metal.

Now Karma knew what he was up against he took a more commanding stance, speaking with authority. The rebels stopped talking and whacking their sticks. My friend looked at me with disgust and indicated to the others with a flick of his hand that they should take me to the edge of the camp where I would be out of the way. I was shocked at what was happening. Why was Karma being so mean and dismissive? He was my friend. He would take care of me. Wouldn't he? My mind couldn't even begin to grasp his clever charade. My physical body needed my attention: my legs were shaking so hard I could barely walk, but with a rifle pushed into my back I managed somehow.

I crouched alone at the cliff edge, staring blindly out at the terraced rice fields on the far side of the gorge, wishing I could disappear into the ground. I forced myself to keep calm, taking deep breaths. It felt like my vision was blurring, but then I realised it was already nearly dusk. I knew if Karma and I were to make our escape it would be better if I had some idea of the camp layout, so I looked carefully around me in the fading light. I noticed some small sharp stones near my feet, grabbed them quickly with trembling hands and pushed them deep inside my pockets. Pathetic weapons but they were all I could see.

I could see Karma in the distance, sitting on the grass in the shade of a tree, relaxed. He was telling the rebels a story, and being the children they were they were gathered around him, mesmerised, weapons lying beside them on the grass. For the first time, I started to feel we might have a chance.

A girl approached me. She was hardly distinguishable from her male fellows, with the same thin, wiry body and ragged uniform. I had heard that girls were recruited and trained to kill, just like the boys. The younger ones were used as messengers, cooks and porters, and paid in food, but it didn't look like this girl had eaten in days. She couldn't have been more than 12 years old although her half-starved body made her look even younger. She circled me a few times, scrutinising me from every angle, then stared into my blue eyes without blinking. She might have held my gaze forever had she not been summoned by one of her comrades. As she walked away she turned and spat at me.

Now I was alone again I forced myself to concentrate, mentally recalling the route we had taken, etching a map in my mind. I hated being cut off from Karma and prayed fervently that he had a plan. I knew no one would come looking for us and I berated myself again for my foolishness in insisting on setting out without letting anyone know when we were due to arrive at our destination. We were a long way from the safety of a town and miles from the nearest army outpost. There was nowhere we could run. If we were to get out of here I knew we would need the bike.

Karma's group were growing louder. They were drinking *rakshi*, a home-brewed firewater that stripped your throat raw. The girls had started a fire. I shivered in my lonely spot and drew my scarf up to cover most of my face. A heavy mist rolled over the mountains. I had used up my last drop of adrenalin and my body was limp with fatigue. Night set in, the sky turned inky black.

It was bitterly cold. I reckoned it must be 2 am. My eyes strained to pick out anything in the darkness. What was Karma doing? The camp was quiet. Desperate for a pee, I felt my way on my hands and knees to a tree and went behind it. As I did so bursts of automatic gunfire split the air, explosions shaking the ground. I could smell smoke and burning rubber. There was the sound of running feet and screeching, which broke into peals of raucous laughter. I breathed again.

Reportedly, no foreigner had ever been killed by the rebels, although many had been asked for donations at gunpoint. Somehow I could not see this mob of stragglers being organised enough to use me as PR to wake up the international community. It was much more likely I would be killed by a stray bullet from one of these drunken kids' guns. I rolled onto my back on the damp grass and stared up at the murky sky. I must have fallen asleep.

The next thing I knew I was being shaken awake. I felt warm breath on my cheek and inhaled the strong smell of *rakshi*. Karma spoke softly into my ear. 'Quick! Get up. Don't ask questions.'

He held my hand firmly as we slowly and carefully crept through the camp. I held my breath and willed my heart to still. Karma moved in the darkness with the confidence of a cat. The bike was where we had left it. I prayed that no one had drained the fuel from the tank. We would only have a split second to find out.

'Get on,' he whispered. 'Don't worry, I drive better when I'm drunk.'

I climbed on behind Karma and, with his sharp downward thrust on the starter, the motor roared. We had no time to look over our shoulders but scrambled, zigzagging, through the forest, skidding on the mossy paths. Branches tore at my hair. Karma didn't dare put on the headlight. Gunshots blasted through the air. We heard screams of fury, but we didn't stop to look back. I steeled myself for a bullet, but mercifully none hit home.

After crashing through the foliage, we bumped down onto a paved road and zipped past a burnt-out police station, the headlight picking out walls plastered with Maoist graffiti: red hammer-and-sickle flags and 'Long Live People's War' splashed in black paint. Karma drove until the tank was nearly empty. We didn't speak. Dawn was breaking now and there were a few signs of life. We passed an overladen truck with six men standing on the bumper and a group of early risers drinking tea. It was a comfort to see the world ticking over as usual.

We stopped for a liquid breakfast at a roadside café—a couple of shots of cheap Indian whisky. Alcohol was our saviour now, as I realised it had been the night before. I thought my relief was going to explode in floods of tears, but when I looked at Karma we both burst out laughing...and were unable to stop.

Leadership lesson #2

Sometimes we are tested to demonstrate our trust. Absolute trust means intentionally letting yourself fall, knowing someone will be there to catch you. It means no reservations, no secret safety net, even if the idea scares us to death, and no elaborate plans or preparations—just an exhilarating jump into the unknown. This is a common enough experience when we are children, innocent and open, but much rarer in our adult lives, unless we are into extreme sports.

***

Experiment now so you will be game ready when the time comes for you to prove your trust. For a leader, this may mean ceding control, trusting your team, recognising and encouraging their abilities and potential. Think about a relationship, whether personal or professional, that is important to you.

- Do you sometimes take control when it would be better to let someone else lead?
- When can you begin to take the risk of trusting someone?
- What does it feel like to trust them implicitly?

When was the last time you stuck your head above the parapet?

3

Be the voice

How frustration and failure turned to influence after Cyclone Yemyin in Pakistan

Seven months after the October 2005 earthquake in Pakistan, many of the affected communities were beginning to get back on their feet, but others were still suffering badly. The last thing anyone needed was another disaster. Then on 23 June 2007, Cyclone Yemyin tore through Sindh and Balochistan provinces, followed by torrential rain and catastrophic flooding. Many villages were completely marooned, with roads and railway lines blocked by landslides; water systems and wells were destroyed, along with houses, crops and livestock beyond number. Nearly four hundred thousand people lost their homes, with hundreds dead or missing. And to make matters worse, the weather pattern was set to continue for another two to three months.

In Islamabad, intense storms had for weeks turned the streets into muddy rivers of swirling debris. Moving around the city was difficult, but it was nothing compared with the images we had seen of the cyclone-affected area: families perching on the roofs of mosques or in trees; people wading through waist-deep water, suitcases balanced on their heads. I knew I needed to get to the area, quickly.

The government of Pakistan had chosen not to broadcast an appeal for international assistance. Foreign journalists were told to stay away, so the news getting through was patchy. To make matters worse, international charities were also asked not to travel to the disaster areas, which they badly needed to do in order to assess the situation. As I was employed at that time by a national Pakistani NGO funded by the World Bank, the directive didn't actually apply to me. I went straight to the charity's director, requesting their backing. I wanted to conduct an assessment mission to evaluate the needs of the victims and see how we might help. He was used to me by then, and thankfully I was given the green light.

On July 19, I landed in Sukkur and was met at the airport by Mahdi, who worked for a local Sindhi NGO and had elected to be my guide. I had heard about Mahdi on the charity grapevine. He was well liked and admired for his 20 hard years of service. Although his faith in what he was doing had been battered over time, and he had little belief that his charity's achievements would be sustainable over the long term, he slogged on diligently, never giving up. Over the months I got to know Mahdi I never failed to marvel at how hard and unstintingly he worked. A man with a big heart.

'Linda, it's terrible. The aid isn't getting through quickly enough.' He gave my arm a squeeze. We didn't hug—it was too hot for that. I was already cursing my headscarf and long-sleeved top. 'It will reach nearly 50 degrees by lunchtime. The flood victims are camped out on any piece of high ground they can find. No shade at all. Can you imagine?' He opened the car door for me. 'Excuse the mess. I've been living in it for days.'

The backseat was packed to bursting: a jumble of water bottles, first aid supplies and food leftovers. The smell was rancid but Mahdi seemed to be oblivious to it. He had more important things on his mind.

'Where are we going first?' I asked, climbing into the front.

'If the roads are not yet submerged, we'll hopefully get as far as Dadu and Shahdadkot,' he said. 'First I want you to get a full briefing from my army contacts.'

We sped off along a highway. I expected to see lines of relief trucks heading in the same direction, but the roads were eerily deserted.

After a while, on either side the fields started to disappear under the floodwater. Soon our single raised road was the only structure in sight. It was as if the Arabian Sea had burst inland.

Mahdi was filling me in on the situation. 'The people are angry. It's not a pretty picture,' he warned me. 'Riots are breaking out all over. They're desperate for aid. Water supplies are contaminated and there's no electricity.'

I looked up at the blackening sky and wondered how much more rain it would take before the road itself was devoured. I shuddered, wondering how deep the water was. The odd corn stalk poked its head above the surface, the only sign there had been a crop growing here.

I grabbed my camera. 'I've got to record it all, Mahdi. Please remind me if I forget to take pictures. It's really important.'

At a makeshift army base we met Captain Walim, who was bent over a map with his fellow Pakistani rangers when we drove up. A tall man in khaki and a wide-brimmed hat, he was tracing lines with a stick and giving orders. He straightened when we walked up. He asked me to sit down.

'What are you doing here?' He wasn't hostile, but definitely suspicious. 'Journalist?'

'No,' I replied. 'I'm working for a local charity, based in Islamabad.'

Mahdi stepped forward, speaking to the captain in Urdu. As he explained, the other man's face softened a little.

'Okay, young lady. Here it is.' I got out my notepad to take notes. 'We're battling against the floodwater. It's moving south from Dadu at speed—it's already covered 25 kilometres. My men are trying to keep one step ahead to evacuate people in its path, but it's almost impossible. So many people are getting stranded on the bunds.'

He showed me the map, pointing out where the bunds, or levees, had been sufficient to hold back minor floods, but they were quite inadequate for something on this scale. 'Right across this area,' he said. 'All of them. Washed away.'

'Can you advise us where we should be visiting today?' I asked him.

The captain spoke to one of his men, then turned to us.

'Follow Corporal Sheeha,' he said. 'He'll take you there. I'd keep it brief if I were you. The sun is a killer. It's bad enough in daylight. After dark it's treacherous—and riots are breaking out everywhere.'

We promised we'd be back by nightfall.

Corporal Sheeha was a short, stout man with a John Wayne swagger who seemed delighted to be coming with us. I felt instantly at ease with him.

'Let's go. Stay close to me.'

He jumped into a big green army truck and we followed in Mahdi's car, keeping close, bumper to bumper. Soon the already narrow road became even narrower as makeshift shelters on either side jostled for space. It was a pitiful sight. We came to a halt beside two baby girls who had been placed under a ragged sheet draped over two wooden bed-frames turned on their sides. The girls stared into space unblinking, legs as fragile as twigs. Next to their shelter, a dead infant lay between the wheels of an upturned cart.

'Take a picture,' said Mahdi. 'Let them see how dreadful it is.'

We moved slowly along the track, witnessing one dire scene after another. Family after family, crouched, hiding from the baking sun any way they could. Up ahead I could just make out a man in the water up to his nose. Somehow he was still managing to wade along, his right hand stretched high above his head holding the last of his possessions: his sandals.

Turning a sharp corner the army truck came to an abrupt halt. Mahdi and I jumped out of the car to see what had happened. The road ahead had crumbled under the pressure of water. There were at least 10 metres missing. On the other side, families, carts and men on bicycles were gathered, marooned.

Corporal Sheeha reached for his walkie-talkie. 'This must have just happened. I must alert Captain Walim.'

The crowd was screaming, jumping up and down and waving their arms. The corporal raised a hand, indicating to them to wait, be calm. I grabbed Mahdi's arm. A man had leapt into the water in a frantic attempt to swim the gap. He had no chance. In seconds he was dragged downstream by the fast-flowing water. I breathed again when I saw that he had managed to grab hold of a tree branch.

Corporal Sheeha shouted to the man. 'Hold on! You'll have help soon!'

He turned to us. 'Captain Walim is sending our one and only hydrofoil. It should be here soon.'

We stood at the water's edge, feeling helpless.

The corporal checked to see I was okay. 'Please go and drink some water,' he said kindly. 'It looks like you're about to faint.'

I did as I was told. Soon I made out the growing hum of the hydrofoil.

'Let's go,' the corporal said. 'Under control now.' It looked far from that to me. Dodging the ever-growing crowd who were watching the rescue, we reversed a kilometre and turned off onto an even narrower side road. The sights continued to appal me. Occasionally we would slow down to allow a trail of barefoot women and children to pass. They did not even turn to look at us but moved along slowly, faces a mask of pain and despair. Many of them carried an infant on their hip and on their heads were huge bundles: pots and pans, a bag of rice, bedding. We peered at them through the shimmering heat haze.

We passed a boat full of men, who were standing so as to cram in as many as possible. It was barely above the water line.

'Mahdi,' I said. 'That boat doesn't have a single woman or child on board.' I felt outraged. They had left their women and children to fend for themselves. 'Slow down. I need to take a picture.'

The men suddenly noticed me and whistled and cheered lecherously. My blood boiled. A little further along we stopped.

'This is the end of the road. We walk from here,' the corporal told us. 'Captain Walim wants you to see where the people are stranded on bunds. Still with no shelter. We can't get tents or water to them fast enough.'

I braced myself for the next circle of hell. As we walked, painfully thin boys came to join our group, running and screaming and circling around us. Soon there were fifty or so following. The pied piper had arrived.

Corporal Sheeha was amused. 'You've caused quite a stir. Nice to see them animated for a while.'

Finally we reached a makeshift medical tent. 'We cannot move anyone for the moment so we've brought doctors and social workers here,' the corporal said. Inside there were six camp beds, each occupied by a patient hooked up to an IV drip. Around the tent a crowd of hungry, bewildered people hung about.

'Stand back, please,' the corporal commanded. 'Let the sick get some air.' The crowd edged back reluctantly. He led me into the tent. 'Come and meet Dr Azam.'

I waited as the doctor performed the difficult task of inserting an IV drip into the back of a severely dehydrated boy's hand. His body was in a state of collapse, with no veins visible. Dr Azam tried many times before he succeeded. It must have been painful for the boy, but he didn't move or cry, just stared with glazed eyes at the needle and bandage strapped to his sparrow-like hand. He was so badly malnourished that although he was probably four years old, he looked no more than two.

'Come and sit in the shade,' Dr Azam said, handing the limp child back to his mother. 'I need a break.'

Dr Azam looked at the end of his rope. His face was haggard and he was pencil thin. His unwashed hair was sticking to his scalp and his clothes were stained with a combination of blood, dirt and sweat.

'We're doing our best,' he said, 'but it's not enough. Our biggest problem is the lack of clean drinking water. You saw the boy.' He explained that the children's bodies had little strength to ward off diarrhoea, dysentery, respiratory diseases or malaria. 'Trouble is, they were already half-starved before the floods.'

'How many of them are orphans?' I asked.

'A lot,' he replied. 'Only the lucky few managed to scramble onto the bank when 10 feet of water rushed in. Many were swept away.'

Dr Azam gazed helplessly at the growing crowd outside the medical tent. 'It's only going to get worse. When the flood recedes, the stagnant water will bring malaria. And more snakebite.'

'We'll have to get you more help by then,' said Mahdi.

A young social worker came over. Wrapped like a mummy in many layers of cloth, she must have been unbearably hot. She handed Dr Azam a bottle of water. He thanked her wearily.

'There aren't many women in the queue,' I said. 'Why is that?'

'Mahdi, you'll need to take Linda to see the women.' He turned to me. 'They're the most vulnerable of all. You'll see.'

The doctor pulled himself up and we said goodbye. He was the only medic here and was working round the clock. I couldn't bear to think what would happen if he got sick. We wished him luck.

Mahdi and I walked on slowly without speaking. The heat bore down on us, a hammer driving into our skulls. I loosened my *hijab*. My throat was bone dry, but with so many people around me desperate for water it didn't feel right to take out my bottle. A little way ahead I could see a small island of mud bulging out like a carbuncle from the main bund. On it was what looked like a discarded heap of colourful clothes. As we drew closer I realised it was a group of women and children huddled together on the dirt, with no shade at all.

Mahdi told me that physical hardship was only part of their problem. 'They're so traumatised at being visible. The whole family honour is wrapped up in their keeping *purdah*. Being shut away.'

We approached the group cautiously. They were clearly terrified, washed up by the floodwater and left at the side of the road like so much flotsam to be picked over by passers-by. Never having been seen by men outside their family, they bowed their heads and hid their faces.

Mahdi spoke soothingly. 'We are here to help you. Please do not be afraid.'

The group huddled even closer, but two of the older women stood up. One of them stepped forward. Her cheekbones stuck out sharply from her sunken face. She looked like one of the walking dead.

Her voice was thin but she radiated anger. 'Look at us! I am a widow. My children have no food.'

Mahdi spoke to the woman in Urdu, then translated for me. 'She says that when the truck came yesterday she wasn't strong enough to fight for her ration. The men got it all.'

The other woman spoke in a trembling voice. 'We are scared for the safety of our children, especially the girls. We hear stories. Children going missing in the night.'

I looked at the women. Some of them were pregnant. I thought what a hellish situation it was for them, or for those menstruating. No water, no sanitation.

Mahdi spoke calmly in a strong voice. He told the women that he, personally, would come back the next day with tents and ration packs. Each pack would contain enough rice, ghee, candles, soap and water purification tablets to keep them going. The women nodded their thanks.

'*Inshallah*, you will return.' They stood like statues, watching us leave.

'Come on,' Mahdi said. 'We need to hurry if we're to get back before dark.'

By the time we reached Corporal Sheeha my head was throbbing. 'You don't look at all well,' he said, fussing over me like a mother hen. 'Time to get some fluids into you.' He looked at the sky. 'Rain's on the way. We need to get going.' As we set off, the rain started.

Very soon it was a torrent and our windscreen wipers were useless against it. Mahdi huddled over the wheel, peering through the blur of rainwater. We were making almost no progress. Heading in the opposite direction, a convoy of water tankers, trucks and tractors, loaded with sacks, bedding and mattresses, was making its way to the flood survivors. Going our way, in an exodus of misery, were those determined to leave the devastated area. We crawled along behind an old wooden cart piled high with the remnants of people's lives: clothes, cooking pots and bedding. Women and children, drenched to the skin, perched precariously on top. I wondered if we were the last vehicle to get through: all the time the fragile roads were crumbling under the pressure of water.

When we reached the army base, Captain Walim was waiting for us. He wasn't happy.

'You should have been back hours ago, Corporal,' he said. 'What were you thinking?'

Before the other man could answer I spoke up. 'I'm sorry. It was our fault. The good news is we've got the pictures. We've seen enough.' I told him that Mahdi would drive me straight back to Karachi, where I would take the first flight to Islamabad. Then to the World Bank for a debrief. 'This needs to be told.' I said. 'I promise, your help won't have been wasted.'

Captain Walim was torn. He was keen to see me off his patch, but he also felt responsible. 'You're crazy,' he said. 'It's an eight-hour drive from here to Karachi.'

He looked out from under the tent canopy at the rain sheeting down in the darkness. 'We've just had news it's happened again. Kashmore district is now under water. Should have been safe. Surrounded by bunds.'

Mahdi asked what had happened. It seemed that a government minister had ordered his people to cut a hole in one of the bunds to stop his own land getting inundated. The villagers were given only two hours' notice to pack their things and clear out before the bund was breached.

I looked at the captain, shocked. He shrugged his shoulders. 'That's life,' he said. 'Survival of the fittest.'

We drove slowly for hours. I was worried Mahdi might fall asleep at the wheel. I looked out at the straggly lines of people and animals trudging through the rain: farmers with a buffalo or two, searching in vain for a scrap of pasture on which they could graze, shepherds with shotguns strapped to their backs for protection against bandits.

We finally reached the city and I shuttled to Islamabad. The director of the World Bank immediately started issuing instructions. 'Before we do anything else, we need to show this to Parliament, give the presentation to the General in Charge of Relief at the NDMA [National Disaster Management Authority]. Let's hear what he has to say. Then we can plan what to do.' He turned to his PA. 'Frida, please call the general. Say it's urgent. We need a meeting within the hour.'

I went to the bathroom and splashed cold water on my face. If it hadn't been for the adrenalin coursing through my system, I didn't think I would have got this far.

Less than an hour later we arrived at the NDMA and I gave my slide show to the general and his disaster relief team. When the general had viewed the last image he turned to me. 'When were these taken?'

'Yesterday,' I said. I kept my voice calm. There was no need for histrionics — the photos said it all.

I waited in the room with the three World Bank officials while the general talked with his colleagues outside. When he returned he spoke to us with evident sincerity.

'Thank you,' he said. 'It's very clear that we need to get extra relief to the area. We'll get onto it at once.' As we left he shook my hand warmly. 'I will keep you all informed.'

A week later, at the Pearl Continental Hotel in Karachi, the same slide show was played to a room packed with business leaders. National and multinational companies were there in force, including Standard Chartered Bank, ICI, Unilever, DuPont, iTextiles, Citibank, Telenor and Engro. They all wanted to help, to play a part in the emergency relief effort. Everyone was buzzing with ideas: the pharmaceutical companies discussed which medicines they should send first; the mobile phone companies suggested how they could boost communication in the area. Each company decided how they could use their core business to help to mobilise food rations, tents, water and other essentials.

At the end of the session the director of the World Bank stood up. 'Linda went to the heart of the disaster,' he said. 'She took enormous personal risk in order to bring us this presentation. It's not her people, not her country. The least we can do is help.'

Leadership lesson #3

Often we do not have the power or resources to do all we would wish to effect positive change in a difficult and complex situation. We feel frustrated, helpless, as though we've failed. That's not acceptable. There is always something in our toolbox we can use. Our voice—speaking up—can be a big part of the solution.

***

Sometimes you will find yourself in a situation in which you know you have to speak up, that your voice can make a real difference: only you were there; only you know what needs to be done. The responsibility is huge and daunting.

- What is it you need to speak up about?

- Who are you helping by not speaking up?

- When was the last time you acknowledged someone else's bravery when they stepped up or stood up for others?

Flood refugees, Sindh Province, Pakistan

Can showing weakness really build strength?

4

Facing fear

How I was brought to my knees on a mountainside in Nepal—and discovered excellence

The frontline of major disasters has been my office for nearly two decades, and here my role is always that of leader. I aim to inspire others with my passion and to be their cheerleader when things get difficult. When others falter, I become tough and resilient. On the frontline I find I have the courage and clarity to make hard decisions—I am super strong.

Just over a year ago, I was leading a team to Thangdor, a remote mountain village in Nepal hit hard by the 2015 earthquake. My local Nepali team had learned about the widespread devastation suffered by the village through the network of Sherpas who climb the remote Himalayas for a living. We knew that many villagers had died and most of the survivors had lost homes and livelihoods. No aid had yet touched this village, so we were on a mission to reach these forgotten people.

Earlier that morning, together with my small trusted team, I had left Kathmandu by jeep and began the slow and hazardous journey to Thangdor. The few sealed sections of road quickly disappeared, and miles of rough track and sheer mountainous drops lay ahead. I was familiar with the route, but the earthquake had turned what had been a beautiful, awe-inspiring journey into a horrifying ordeal. The devastation throughout the region was immeasurable. Everywhere we looked homes and temples had been razed to the ground and a sense of loss and despair was evident in every village. The jeep bounced and rocked wildly from side to side as our driver negotiated the huge boulders, collapsed buildings and abandoned vehicles in our path. When we finally reached our first destination, we had been on the road for eight hours.

My team immediately jumped out of the vehicle and scanned the wide horizon. Bruised and exhausted, I eased myself out of the jeep and stretched, fondly imagining that in just a few moments I would be enjoying a soothing hot cup of chai in the village. Then I noticed the anxious looks being exchanged by the Sherpas, and my heart sank. What I hadn't yet appreciated was that a huge landslide had completely blocked the road ahead. Boulders the size of cars had plunged down the mountainside, creating an impenetrable barrier. We didn't know it then, but it would be nine months before the road reopened, compounding this village's isolation.

'What now?' I asked Namgel, our Sherpa guide. 'Do we retrace our steps and find another way in?'

'No, this is the only way.' He pointed towards a distant spot on the horizon. 'We must continue on foot.'

I tried to gauge the route we would have to take as I gazed down at the gorge far below and then up to the distant craggy rock Namgel was pointing to. The 'only way' was steep and covered in scree and rubble from the landslide. No obvious track, and nothing to stop us from falling once we lost our footing.

I had never been fond of heights, and now my brain and body screamed, *I can't do this!* I was frozen to the spot, praying that someone would conjure up an alternative solution. I could feel a cold sweat beginning to form on my forehead.

Namgel interrupted my thoughts. 'Let's go, Linda. There's no other way.'

'I can't,' I heard a small voice say.

Namgel approached me and quietly and calmly assured me that, yes, I could do it.

Namgel has been in my Nepali team for many years. He is a highly experienced Sherpa and guide and has led hundreds of treks into the Himalayas. Responding to his encouragement, I reached into the jeep and grabbed my rucksack while quietly giving myself a pep talk. *Come on. The sooner we start, the sooner this will all be over.*

I walked off the track and stepped tentatively onto the steep mountainside, not daring to look further than a few metres ahead. Namgel led the way and for some time I matched his pace, telling myself that if I trod exactly where he trod, I'd be okay. But every few metres the ground beneath my feet betrayed me and a noisy cascade of rock and dirt had me grasping for a firm anchor. In these moments, I tried not to look down into the valley far below, but it was becoming harder to ignore my growing fear. Time slowed, and although I continued to put one foot in front of the other, it felt as though I wasn't moving and would be trapped on this mountainside forever. Thinking how one false move would send me tumbling helplessly down the mountainside caused the knot in my stomach to tighten. My anxiety was taking physical form: I felt like I could barely breathe, the oxygen pooling in the top of my lungs, my legs shaking uncontrollably.

Focusing on Namgel's back a few metres ahead, I tried to convince myself I had the courage and capacity to make it—*I can do this!* I had seen and coped with so much over the past two decades, it was infuriating to find my body and mind rebelling just when I needed to be calm and focused. I tried to banish my fear but it continued to work its way to the surface, trapped in a torturous loop: *I don't want to die…my children will be so angry…no one will find my body.*

Two hours into the trek I couldn't go on. I was frightened beyond measure. Clinging to the side of the mountain, we had nowhere to sit and rest. Overcome by exhaustion, I broke down and sobbed. Tears streamed down my face. I knew I couldn't take any more.

It was the only time I can remember when fear overwhelmed me.

Namgel retraced his steps. He looked me directly in the eyes, his face showing both concern and understanding. He took my hands and in a calm voice said, 'Linda, take control of your breathing. Breathe in deeply and exhale slowly. Think only about your breathing.' In a fog of fear, I did as I was told and listened as he repeated the words over and over again: 'Breathe in deeply and exhale slowly.' Having unconsciously handed over the role of leader two hours ago, in that moment I surrendered my survival to Namgel. He said, 'You can do this, you know you can. Nothing will happen to you. I am here, and you trust me.'

Finally, with my breathing once more under control, Namgel changed his tone to one of quiet command: 'We are going to take five paces, and then stop. Are you ready?' I nodded and was surprised to find my brain could accept this small, practical and achievable goal. I felt some of Namgel's confidence and calmness course through my body and the knot in my stomach released a little. 'Think of where we are going, Linda. Picture the villagers. They are waiting for us, they need our help. Imagine the faces of the children.'

Namgel's words had an immediate effect. My focus shifted from the fear and pain in my body to the reason we were there, the reason I was on that mountain: to bring help to this remote, suffering village. I stopped thinking about me. None of this was about me. We had a mission, and others were depending on us. With my fear and pain no longer taking centre stage, I could continue the journey—slowly, one foot in front of the other.

To regain my focus, I began to hum one of Nepal's favourite songs, 'Resham Firiri', knowing the children would surely be singing it when we reached the village. In my mind I saw them welcoming us with *khatas*, sacred scarves symbolising purity and compassion, and with hugs and *Namaste* all round. I imagined their smiles, their tears, their joy knowing that help had arrived at last, that people cared. *One foot in front of the other, Linda, one foot in front of the other.*

Namgel had found a way to ground me and stop my fear from escalating. Visualising the children who were expecting us enabled me to find the courage and determination to go on, and to push the pain and fear to the back of my mind. It was still there, but now carefully compartmentalised in my head.

It was two more hours before we reached the village. The last hour we fought our way through a torrential hail storm. As we climbed the last peak and finally looked down on the village, a double rainbow appeared. Namgel and I looked at each other and smiled. A sign? We had made it!

On this journey, the leader had become the led. Namgel—Sherpa, guide, friend and salt of the earth—had calmly taken control of the situation. He showed me how to shift my focus from myself, to remember why I was on that mountain, to remember that others were relying on us. He showed me how to control my fear, to stop it reaching the next level, through focused breathing and by breaking the cycle of negative thoughts. Simple but powerful techniques I would use again in the future.

Leadership lesson #4

Knowledge and preparation are power. They build confidence. But sometimes facing the fact that we are not good at everything, and will not succeed at everything, can be hard. So how do we start? How do we face the fear and overcome it? By getting real and recognising and accepting our weaknesses. By choosing a fear to work on and taking baby steps towards embracing and overcoming it. By intentionally changing the way we think about it.

***

Recognise your strengths, where people call on you most, but be humble enough to acknowledge when you don't have the answers and to ask for help.

- Do you trust and delegate to others at times when you may not be the best person to lead?

- How could your vulnerability actually help you to build a strong team?

- What of yourself would you be willing to share with others?

Be The Change: Business leaders on the frontline,
Himalayas, Nepal

Have you ever made
unfounded assumptions—and
paid a heavy price?

5

Know the context

How I failed to anticipate cultural difference in my transition from Thailand to Pakistan

I was sitting with my team of business leaders in Bangkok when I first heard about the earthquake in Pakistan in October 2005. The news was just coming through and we listened to it together. 'Right, you'll be off then, Linda,' Simon said. How well he knew me!

I was naive to think that Pakistan would be anything like Thailand. Did I think I could dive in, do the job and leave to a chorus of friendly cheers? Perhaps. I would soon know better. The energetic community spirit that was so apparent in Thailand, and extended even to foreigners, seemed barely to exist in Pakistan. There, as it turned out, supplies sent to the disaster area were often as not looted before they reached the families in desperate need. With their employers unable to vouch for their safety, foreign journalists and aid workers were being sent home in droves. Kidnappings, suicide bombs, mob killings. It wasn't a good place to be. Westerners felt especially unwelcome in Pakistan, and if you were white and female you were the guest no one wanted at their table.

My first mistake was arriving at the airport on my own. I hadn't organised any official transport. It wasn't an oversight—I like to see a situation for myself without being insulated behind a layer of protection.

For the same reason, I had chosen a local guesthouse rather than a large hotel. What I didn't realise was that by doing so I was putting myself and others in danger.

I walked out onto the airport concourse, to be confronted by a large crowd. I felt hundreds of eyes staring at me with laser-like intensity and understood how Beckham must feel walking out onto the pitch at Wembley Stadium. For a moment I wondered if my skirt was tucked into my knickers, but of course what set me apart was my pale skin and blond hair. Not an inch of flesh showed below my high-necked top, but I still caused a stir. Unable to see the exit, or a way through the crowd, I began to feel a bit panicky. Then, hearing the magic cry of 'Taxi!', I set off briskly in its direction.

The sea of white *shalwar kameez* parted miraculously, and I hurried through the gap. I still felt a little dazed as the taxi driver approached me.

'Where are you going, miss?'

'I need to get to this guesthouse.' I handed him a crumpled piece of paper on which was scribbled the address.

He took it and, without stopping to glance at the address, ushered me quickly to his car. Inside it there were no door or window handles. I looked at the dashboard. No meter.

'What's your rate? How much will…?'

The driver, a tall man who had folded himself behind the wheel of his tiny Suzuki with surprising agility, cut me off in mid sentence.

'Listen, miss. I will take you to your guesthouse.' He looked at me, unsmiling. 'You are lucky to have me as your taxi driver. A woman travelling alone. It's dangerous.'

He told me to sit in the middle, keeping away from the windows. I had the feeling that this was as much for his safety as for mine. We wove our way through brightly painted, jingling trucks that belched out thick black smoke. Carts laden with melons, local buses crammed with passengers, more bodies hanging by their fingertips from the window frames and ledges — ordinarily, I would have delighted in the chaotic scene, but the taxi driver's dark warning had dampened my spirits. But it wasn't just that. I had found the atmosphere oppressive from the moment I got off the plane. Why? What was it? I'd been all over the world and had never had quite this feeling, as if I was in a truly alien place.

As the cab jerked along, braking often to avoid children selling cigarettes to the drivers, the answer dawned on me: there were no women. No grandmas, wives, little girls. And I couldn't recall having seen any from the moment I walked out into the airport concourse. The taxi driver dropped me off at the guesthouse and drove away quickly. My welcome wasn't much warmer inside. The manager seemed equally disturbed by having to deal with a woman, travelling alone. I was shown upstairs to a dingy room with peeling walls. I closed the door and sat down on the bed. I couldn't relax. The driver's and manager's jumpiness had rubbed off on me. I got up and pushed a chair under the door handle. 'I'd give anything for a nightcap,' I thought. No such luck.

Next morning the manager could hardly hide his delight when I told him I was leaving. As he said goodbye, I almost heard the words hanging in the air: ... *and don't come back!*

During those first days and weeks in Pakistan there were many times I wanted to cut and run. I was repeatedly advised to leave the country but stubbornly chose to stay on, even when my main sponsor, the International Business Leaders Forum (IBLF), pulled out of the project, unwilling to take further responsibility for my safety. By that time, I had 50 businesses interested in setting up sustainable projects. There was no way I was going to leave.

The 2005 Pakistan earthquake was a disaster on an enormous scale. Thousands were dying of thirst and starvation; families who had lost their homes huddled without shelter under the blistering sun. Aid wasn't reaching them fast enough and what did was pitifully inadequate. Unlike Thailand, the country wasn't a popular holiday destination, so the global media covered the 'story' only briefly. Tsunami aid money kept on flowing, while Pakistan was left to cope almost alone. Thirty thousand square kilometres at the foot of the Himalayas were devastated, many towns and villages simply erased. Before the earthquake much of the population was already living at subsistence level. No one had anything put by for a rainy day. Any crisis and they starved.

I needed to get to the main refugee camp at Balakot. At the bus station in Islamabad, I joined the crowd queuing for the bus. It was my first day in Islamabad and my nerves were still on edge. Absurdly, a Monty Python song, 'I'm a lumberjack and I'm okay', was spinning around in my head. I was horribly aware of being scrutinised forensically by a hundred pairs of eyes. My immediate plan was to do a recce of the earthquake area, but with no escort I was starting to realise that this might not be such a good idea.

Then, a stroke of luck. A white-haired man greeted me with a nod.

'*Assalam aleikum*,' he said. 'Are you off to the earthquake area? Allow me to introduce myself. I am Dr Ghas.'

I realised this was the first time anyone had spoken to me with any warmth since I'd arrived in Pakistan. I told him I was heading for Balakot. He said he would be going that way too, although he was waiting for some medical supplies and wouldn't be there until later.

'Are you waiting for someone?' He glanced around the bus station.

'No, I'm alone.'

At this he looked sombre. He said he hoped I didn't mind some advice. There was something in his tone that made my stomach churn all over again.

'Your bus will make many stops. Sit at the back. When it stops, hide yourself. Bend down below the window so you cannot be seen.'

He paused, understanding my distress. I didn't want to hear this. I didn't want it to be this way. The constant watchfulness, the fatalistic advice. It made me bristle, although I knew the man only wanted to help.

He spoke gently. 'These areas on the north-west frontier are sensitive. The people are very poor, very . . . ' — he searched for the right word — 'emotional. It's best they don't see you're a foreigner.'

'What will they do to me? Throw stones?'

'No. They will kill you.'

I tugged at the scarf around my head, feeling stifled.

'It's okay. I'll speak to the bus driver. I know him. I will say you are my friend.' Dr Ghas told me to get on the bus now. Standing outside any longer would only attract more attention. 'When you get to the camp, go straight to the army base. Ask for the major in charge. Tell him I sent you. Don't talk to anyone else.'

I thanked him and got on the bus, moving to the back. My legs were shaking. I sat down and pulled the grubby curtain across the window, shielding myself from view. I sat for the whole journey huddled, face down, barely moving, feeling afraid every time the bus stopped.

I was met at the bus stop in Balakot by one of Dr Ghas's friends, a man called Gullam. Dr Ghas had called him while I was on the bus, suggesting he take me on a tour of the worst-hit areas. We would then wait for the doctor at an agreed spot on the way to a place called Mitakot.

Gullam drove slowly, skirting rubble and wide cracks in the road. As far as I could see, in every direction, were piles of grey rocks and huge gaping craters. It looked like the surface of the moon.

'Balakot was where the two plates collided. They tell me the mountains moved sideways. The earth moved upwards with a jolt. Then crashed down.'

'There's nothing left,' I said, half to myself.

'It was a beautiful city.'

We waited in silence for Dr Ghas on the mountain road. He arrived in an ancient green army jeep, tooting the horn with a flourish.

'I finally managed to get us a ride. Almost impossible to find a driver.'

The one he had managed to find had a very nasty limp. He'd had a metal rod put in his leg and only used one foot on the pedals. He never once used his brakes, only the clutch, even on the tightest of bends. I wondered if we would make it to Mitakot.

We drove for over an hour, climbing constantly. I couldn't see a single house left standing. When we got out it was freezing cold and raining. I was thankful for my walking boots as the ground was covered with rubble. Finally we reached some makeshift shelters, a few tents and tarpaulins, some drapes woven together.

Dr Ghas called out, 'Assalam aleikum.'

A tall thin man with a speckled beard appeared from a shelter, behind him a few male villagers. He was wrapped in thick white blankets. On his head an Afghan turban. He didn't say anything, just stood there for an age, staring.

Dr Ghas broke the silence. 'We are here to help. I am a doctor.'

The man moved forward to greet us. He led us through what remained of their homestead. The men had lost everything—families, homes and livestock. He told us that the buffalo had been crushed in their stalls. Every last chicken had been killed when the henhouse collapsed.

'We haven't had people up here. The weather has been too bad.'

They knew they couldn't rebuild before winter set in and were resigned to living in the tents. They didn't know if they would survive. I had heard that truckloads of blankets, sleeping bags and warm clothes, earmarked for the earthquake survivors, were being sold in the local markets.

We walked silently behind the villagers. There was nothing to say. We were led to the one remaining shelter and there Dr Ghas patiently listened as each man voiced his needs. I watched their faces as they spoke, gaunt with worry. I could hear but not see the women, whispering in the shadows at the back of the tent.

Eventually Dr Ghas said we had to go. 'It's getting late. We need to get back before dark.'

He told the men that he would return each week to check how they were doing physically. In the meantime he would make sure that dry food rations, tents and blankets were sent up.

It took us half an hour to get through the army checkpoints and into the camp. We were body searched and our documents checked several times. By now it was getting late. We were shown into an army tent and told to wait for the major.

When he arrived he wasn't pleased. 'What is she doing here?' virtually spitting the words.

Dr Ghas spoke to him quickly in Urdu.

The major turned to me, red-faced with anger. 'Don't you know there is a curfew? It's for your own safety. You shouldn't be here.'

I stammered that I didn't know.

'I am sorry. I didn't know either,' Dr Ghas said. 'Look, where can she stay? It's too late to set out now.'

The major's anger seemed to drain away abruptly—he had more pressing concerns. 'Bridges and roads are collapsed. We've no hospitals, and on top of that there's looting and fighting breaking out everywhere.' He wiped his face with his sleeve, exhausted. 'I'm sorry. Both army and refugee camps are off limits. No foreigners.'

Dr Ghas looked worried. There was nothing to say so we took our leave.

'Linda, it's too dangerous to drive now. Too many thieves and bandits on the roads.'

'I am so sorry to be such a problem. What choices do we have?'

With no hotels left standing within a 50-mile radius we had only one option. Dr Ghas led me to a concrete house that belonged to a friend of his. The top floor had collapsed, its roof resting on the earth. It was a tangled mess of broken glass, metal beams and rubble.

'Wait here,' he said. 'I'll see if any part of it is safe.'

I'd been told about the frequency of aftershocks. It wasn't surprising that the refugees weren't using the place for shelter. The building was on its last legs. The slightest tremor and it wouldn't stand a chance.

Dr Ghas reappeared, covered in dirt and dust. 'I've found one room that should be okay. Take my arm and watch your step.'

I didn't think I would sleep a wink that night. Dr Ghas had warned me about ghosts. The whole area was full of them, he told me. Next door had been a girls' school. All four hundred students had died, buried alive in the rubble.

'We heard their murmurs for nearly an hour. We dug for days, but not one was rescued.'

I lay down on a broken, damp sofa, covered in fragments of rubble. Shafts of moonlight shone through the gashes in the wall. Dr Ghas, having shared his fears about ghosts, was soon snoring, exhausted. I blessed him silently. Without his help I wouldn't have got through that day.

I lay awake for a long while, offering silent prayers of protection and peace for all those who had suffered. In my hand I gripped a powerful talisman of a revered monk, given to me by some 'sea gypsy' fishermen I had befriended in Thailand.

It was the end of my second day in Pakistan. I knew I had to wise up if I was to be able to take many more.

Leadership lesson #5

Approach every new challenge with fresh eyes. Assumptions are dangerous. To assume that your next experience will be similar to your last is a recipe for disaster. When we assume, we lose our edge, falling into a programmed set of expectations and actions. The leader who moves into a new position or business will be anxious to make an impact early. This may involve implementing a new structure, shifting people around or appointing new staff—all at a run.

Unless you understand the context within which you are working, you won't succeed, and you may cause offence and create waste. A different group, culture, history and set of experiences will produce a totally different context. Taking the time to know the people, what works and what doesn't, will go a long way to ensuring a positive long-term impact.

***

When taking the time to approach and seek to understand new situations, check yourself if you start to make assumptions.

- What assumptions are you making about how things should be?

- What questions do you need to ask that will help you to understand the context more clearly?

- Are you holding back from asking some of these questions? Why?

Are you aware of the hero
who lives within you?

6

Be bold

How extreme spontaneity taught me trust in Nepal

We were travelling on Karma's 200cc trail bike, perfect for speed and the necessary off-roading. The back of that bike was a happy place for me. It brought all my senses to life. I loved being immersed in the elements, feeling the wind and rain, the sun beating down and the chill of the night. I loved being able to look directly into the eyes of passers-by. In a car, I felt like I was watching the world on TV, a detached observer, so I avoided cars whenever possible.

Now we were on our way to visit Aditi in an isolated village perched high on a windswept crag. In our project to help vulnerable Nepali families develop income-generating businesses, Aditi was one of the stars. Starting with an investment of just $100, she had formed a candle-making cooperative, and it was progressing well. She had done her research and tested the market. With daily power cuts of up to 18 hours, every family was obliged to buy candles. Having purchased the necessary moulds, wicks and wax, Aditi could make a candle for 6 Nepali rupees and sell it for 10 rupees. The market was limitless. It was a perfect example of a long-term sustainable business. The number of women joining the cooperative was growing fast.

The women were already gathered waiting for us at the focal point of the village, a magnificent banyan tree. I adored this tree and marvelled at the way its long aerial roots had plunged down from the horizontal branches and taken root to form a forest of trunks from a single tree.

It made my heart sing to see these women so empowered and happy. With limited access to education and medical care, life could be hard in the villages. Extra income gave them food security and put shoes on their children's feet. The women excitedly shared their entrepreneurial stories: where the market was growing, new product ideas. I checked their accounts and we worked on how to grow their market. Where should they sell next? The air was electric.

As dusk approached Karma started to pace up and down. 'We must get back before curfew, Linda. Finish up. It's time to go.' It was hard to pull myself away, though—there was always one more task, one more cup of chai.

'Hop on,' insisted Karma, bringing the bike up alongside me. 'We're leaving.' Reluctantly I waved goodbye to the women.

The track to the village had been carved out of the mountainside. On one side a steep mountain rock face, on the other a sheer cliff drop. It was a precipitous, twisty ride down. Karma, an experienced rider, took the hairpin bends at speed.

This was the time of day I loved. Work done, a beautiful Himalayan vista all around me, misty mountains ranging back as far as the eye could see. Tucked safely behind Karma, I relaxed and gratefully took it all in.

'Cover up,' Karma shouted suddenly. I sat up straight and looked over his shoulder. In the distance I saw figures walking along the cliff side of the road. They were small—they looked like children. 'Maoists.' Karma's voice was tense and clipped.

I could now make out the distinct red scarf that some tied around their head like a bandana, symbolising their willingness to die for the cause. I held my breath. *What now?* I wondered. There was nowhere to turn, nowhere to hide. Instinctively I tried to shrink into invisibility on the back of the bike (not easy for a blond woman of 5 feet, 11 inches). I pulled my hood up and my scarf over my mouth and nose, and yanked at my jacket sleeves to try to cover my hands.

Karma maintained a steady speed as we moved past the first boy soldier. The boy's head was drooped, his clothes dirty, rifle hanging loosely across his chest, too exhausted even to look up at us as he struggled up the steep hill. My heart went out to him, and I wondered when he had last eaten.

Karma was silent as we rounded the next bend, but I felt him gasp. A half a mile in front of us a stationary bus was parked close to the steep cliff edge. Boy soldiers were streaming off the bus, filling the narrow gap between the bus and the cliff. An officer could be heard shouting, '*Jaldi, Jaldi*' (Hurry up!).

My heart sank. Karma had no choice but to stop. It was all over. They would take me and most likely punish him severely. I squeezed his arm in acceptance and whispered, 'It's all right my friend, there's nothing you can do.'

Suddenly I was thrown backwards. Karma had opened up the throttle and we were racing at breakneck speed straight at the back of the bus. *This is suicide!* I thought. I clung on, bracing for the impact. At the last moment Karma swerved to point the bike at the tiny gap between bus and cliff. He yelled and the boys threw themselves out of our way. It was chaos, the noise terrible, the boys screaming in panic as we roared through. My heart was pounding so hard it felt it would burst through my chest. I squeezed my eyes tight to shut it all out, opening them for a split second just as we passed the door of the bus. I was looking right into the shocked eyes of the officer.

We sped on. Gunshots echoed loudly through the mountains. Head down, Karma drove like the wind around the next bend, and the next.

We didn't speak.

After what seemed like hours Karma finally slowed and pulled up in front of a chai shop. 'Go inside, Linda,' he said gently. 'I'll put the bike around the back.'

Inside, Karma called for two large pegs of brandy.

My mouth was so dry with fear I could hardly get the words out. 'How did you find the courage to do that, Karma?'

He smiled as he threw down his 60 ml peg in one gulp and called for another. 'I had no intention of losing you.'

I reached out and squeezed his hand. 'Thank you, my friend. You saved my life.'

'Enough,' Karma said. 'We are a team,' adding with his signature twinkle, 'so what's our next mission?'

Leadership lesson #6

Sometimes, when there is no time for deliberation, you need to find the courage to take a calculated risk. A hero is a person who acts selflessly even in the most testing circumstances. A hero is not *without* fear but rather does what is right *in spite of* fear.

Most people don't succeed as they might because they are afraid of failure. No hero is perfect. We all make mistakes, but that doesn't invalidate the contributions we make in the course of a life in which we test ourselves.

***

Have the courage to trust your gut and take the risk. Be daring. Try saying *yes* to things on impulse. Don't plan too much. Expect nothing and be ready for everything.

- Do you ever demand more of yourself than others would expect?

- Do you feel comfortable being spontaneous, or are you afraid of failure?

- Do you sometimes throw yourself into a situation without taking time to rationalise it? What is usually the outcome?

Part II

Passion

The two most important days in your life are the day you
are born and the day you find out why.

Mark Twain

How often do you take
the time to reach beyond
superficial chat to really get
to know someone?

7
Meaningful connection

How I learned the meaning of true connection from HH the Dalai Lama

My extraordinary friendship with the Tibetan people began in 2001 when for six months I travelled the length and breadth of India visiting remote and scattered Tibetan refugee camps. The problems faced by the young people in these camps had become so serious that His Holiness the Dalai Lama himself was keen to hear the results of my research. That meeting was to have an extraordinary influence on my life.

On Saturday, 26 October 2002, I travelled to Mindrolling Monastery, near Dehradun in India's north-west. I was greeted by the sight of a joyous carnival, a bobbing sea of burgundy and saffron. A throng of monks, meditating and reciting sutras to the musical accompaniment of sacred horns and cymbals, had gathered to catch a glimpse of this revered man of peace.

Inside the monastery I was taken to an austere office lined with dusty, dilapidated furniture, where I waited for two hours while an Indian official performed the required screening procedures. I sat and watched him move paper documentation painstakingly from one pile to another, pausing a moment to study a page, and occasionally asking me for my signature. This was followed by a close scrutiny of my passport, with a great deal of head-scratching and 'oohs' and 'ahhs'. I understood it was a serious business: the Indian police were responsible for the safety of the Tibetan leader, so it was no wonder I was grilled on my background and reasons for wanting to meet him. As invariably happens when I'm with police or uniformed officials, though, I had an uncontrollable desire to laugh. No matter how hard I tried to control it, every now and again nervous giggles burst out as hiccups.

At last the moment came and I was escorted to His Holiness's private chambers. We waited in a glorious glass conservatory. My senses were almost overwhelmed by the beauty of the place, the enchanting sounds of Tibetan singing bowls and the strong smell of yak butter candles. I felt the power and mysterious symbolism of the *thangkas*, the brocaded paintings hanging on the walls. Through the glass of the conservatory, I could see the glorious gardens outside, in the centre of which was a breathtaking dome-shaped stupa, a dazzlingly colourful and gilded monument some 50 metres high, built to house sacred Buddhist relics.

I stood in that beautiful room, soaking up the moment and not wanting it to end, every cell in my body tingling. In the next room, I could hear the Dalai Lama in audience, his rich, hearty laugh punctuating the conversation. I waited motionless, a white silk scarf or *khata* held in my hands in readiness for his blessing. Quite suddenly the heavy wooden door to his private chamber flew open and the man himself breezed in. I had seen his picture so many times and here he was, in his simple monk's robe, with a grin so wide it seemed to stretch from ear to ear. I was instantly struck by the sheer charisma of the man: he positively glowed with the delight of being alive. He stood directly in front of me, eyes twinkling, his gaze so direct it seemed to reach into my soul. He greeted me playfully, almost boyishly, peeping over his heavy-framed rectangular glasses, eyebrows raised—clearly a man who delighted in meeting new people. Taking my hand in a firm grasp, he held it a while, long enough to make a real connection.

Then he asked me if it was okay for him to take off his shoes. I nodded, surprised by the question, watching as he kicked off his blue plastic flip-flops and sat comfortably cross-legged on the sofa. We sat and he listened intently as I told him about my plans, explaining all about my research project and the many problems faced by the Tibetan youth in exile. As I spoke, he smiled and nodded, often interjecting with a 'well done' or 'very important work'. An hour sped by, both of us totally absorbed in the discussion.

When I happened to mention that I used to be a nurse, the conversation suddenly took a new turn. With the agility of a politician, His Holiness changed tack, as he recognised a resource that could be useful for the cause, that might truly benefit his struggling people. Was there any possibility that I could look into a grave problem within Tibet itself? He explained that Tibet was currently experiencing shockingly high infant mortality rates—and for a moment the smile was gone and he looked grief-stricken. Of course I said I would go anywhere he felt I could best be of help. At that, he leaned over and gave my arm a squeeze. With a beatific smile, he said he would fully support my work. And I realised I'd just been talked into a whole new job!

Realising my audience was nearing its conclusion I dived into my big red carpetbag and pulled out the presents I had selected for him. Choosing a present, particularly one for a man, is never easy at the best of times. But what on earth do you give the self-described 'simple monk' with no need of possessions and no attachment to material things? The question had plagued me for weeks. I had shared it with friends, but none of us had come up with a solution that felt right. I had been brought up always to take a gift when visiting a friend, but—flowers, chocolates? Everything felt ridiculous, yet I knew I could not go empty-handed.

I had rummaged through secondhand bookshops, grabbing any books I could find that covered the young life of the Dalai Lama, hoping to unearth a clue that might inspire me in my search.

'I have a few small gifts for you from England. Can I give them to you now?' I asked.

His Holiness, an avid gardener, examined the selection of old English seed packets, studying them lovingly one by one. He held up the packet of larkspur seeds, announcing excitedly, 'This packet I will send to Ladakh—it will grow particularly well there.'

The next gift, a pen-sized telescope, confused him; he looked quizzically at it for a few moments, then suddenly understood its significance and burst into hysterics. He held it to his eye and told me how, as a child, when he lived high up in the Potala Palace in Lhasa, he used to spy on the soldiers using a telescope.

The final present was a tiny wind-up musical box. In my research I had discovered that another great hobby of His Holiness was to take apart and repair small mechanical items, such as watches and musical boxes. My gift filled the air with music. For a moment we swayed and tapped our feet to the tinny strains of 'Singing in the Rain'. The feeling was magical.

'Now it's time for a photo,' His Holiness exclaimed, beckoning a monk. Without any stiffness or formality he put his arm around me and took my hand in a firm handshake.

After we had bade our farewells I tripped out of the room on cloud nine, and in that moment I think my smile would even have outstretched his own. It felt like every cell in my body was grinning.

Leadership lesson #7

Leadership is quite different from management. People work for a manager; they *follow* a leader. And they will choose to do so when you make a meaningful connection with them. Such a connection can be established only through talking to them, finding out about their lives, their passions.

Show you are curious, take a genuine interest and listen deeply, and you will build a relationship based on mutual respect and understanding. It doesn't have to be a long conversation, but make it meaningful and you will establish a lasting connection.

***

How strong is your web? It's easy to get lost in the business of life and neglect those most important to us. Are you good at keeping in touch with people, or do you drop contacts easily and move on to new ones? Have you stood up for them when they needed you? Think about the people you work with.

- How much do you know about them—their family, hobbies, likes and dislikes?

- How can meaningful connections make your leadership role more fulfilling?

- Is your role narrowly task focused? If so, how is this impacting staff engagement?

Are you a good listener?

8

Listen and learn

How HRH The Prince of Wales became my mentor in the most unlikely setting, a Tibetan refugee camp in Delhi

If you are trying to move mountains it certainly helps to have someone powerful on your side. In the summer of 2002 I was given just the lucky break my Tibet project needed.

Since the 1950s more than 150000 Tibetans had found refuge in India. In contrast to the experience of many refugee communities, money had streamed in from sympathetic donors, and more than half of this was funnelled into education. There were now 106 kindergartens, 87 primary schools, 44 middle schools, 21 secondary schools and 13 senior secondary schools catering to 25000 Tibetan students. Where only 65 per cent of Indian youngsters came out of school able to read and write, more than 90 per cent of Tibetans in India had achieved these skills.

The well-funded, highly organised Tibetan camps had also done a fine job of preserving Tibetan culture, but by isolating themselves from their hosts (the 1.4 billion Indian population could have gobbled them up in a heartbeat), they had created other problems.

Young, well-educated Tibetans led a sheltered life in the camps. Then, at age 18, they were released into the outside world to compete with the more streetwise Indians. There was little vocational training on offer, and unless they became more commercially savvy they hadn't a hope of competing in the job market. With little attempt at integration, they were left to sink or swim. This situation had led to a seemingly endless cycle of disappointment, boredom, substance abuse and suicide.

My project was to research the problem of high drug and alcohol abuse among young people in the Tibetan refugee camps in India and to try to help turn the situation around. I needed to create a bridge, to be a broker between the Indian business world and the many bright, highly educated but despairing young Tibetans. I reached out to Youth Business International in London, one of Prince Charles's charities. They sounded interested in what we were doing. What I didn't know when I phoned was that the Prince of Wales himself would be visiting Delhi that autumn.

When I received a call from the British High Commission suggesting that the Prince should meet some of our Tibetan entrepreneurs, I panicked. Our project was in such a fledgling state that I feared our efforts to impress him would appear derisory and that our young Tibetans might feel exposed. I knew I had to swallow these fears, though. A VIP visit could give the Tibetans just the boost they needed.

Of course I said we would be delighted to receive a visit, and phone calls to London went back and forth for a week or two. Then we hit a snag. Eric, my friend at the British High Commission, called me.

'The Indian government aren't happy,' he said. 'They say it's not safe for the Prince to visit Majnu-ka-tilla.'

'Oh no,' I groaned. I couldn't see how Majnu-ka-tilla, the camp outside Delhi that had been my base throughout my time in India, would pose a threat to his safety.

'That's so unfair,' I said, hot with frustration. 'Dirty and smelly, yes. But not unsafe.'

'They are suggesting you bring the Tibetan entrepreneurs to meet the Prince at a five-star hotel in Delhi,' he said cautiously, anticipating my eruption.

'You know that won't work,' I fired back. 'He needs to see that these businesses are being run from a refugee camp. That's the whole point. They don't live in a bloody five-star hotel!'

I could sense Eric suppressing a smile on the other end of the phone.

'Look, calm down. I've got a suggestion,' he said. 'Some guys from Scotland Yard are coming out on a recce. Let's ask them to assess the site and we can take it from there.'

'And let the Prince decide,' I said. 'Exactly.'

Weeks went by before Eric called me with the news that a group of plainclothes policemen and the Prince's bodyguard and private secretary would be paying us a visit the next day. The visit was quick and efficient. The police spread out to check out the camp and we met up an hour later at the playground, where I planned on showcasing the Tibetan entrepreneurs' work.

Tim, Prince Charles's bodyguard, was relaxed and efficient. 'The Indian government are insisting that we place some armed police on the rooftops,' he said. 'To be honest, I think it's a bit over the top, but we can agree to that. I think the camp will be a good place to visit,' he said. 'The "boss" is keen to meet the refugees on their own turf.'

I breathed out with relief. 'That's wonderful!'

He had a quick word with one of the policemen then turned back to me. 'One last thing,' he said. 'We need to identify a place where you can escort the Prince in an emergency.'

I looked around helplessly. There weren't any rooms that had direct access to the playground. Tim and the policemen walked around the perimeter.

'Hang on. What's this?' Tim opened a small wooden door. He reared back quickly. 'Ah, a rather dirty toilet.' I looked apologetic but he smiled, wiping his hands on his trousers. 'Perfect. If you clean it up it will be fine.'

'Really?' I said with disbelief. Pray God the Prince won't have to go there. I was relieved that the British High Commission had requested the event be very low profile, with few guests and no speeches. The Prince wanted to meet the young people themselves, and for that to happen we couldn't have dozens of officials crowding the place. The press would be allowed to attend but would be kept in one small area.

We had a month to get organised. Five Tibetans were selected to showcase their businesses and products: Pema (beauty treatments); Dawa (event management); Kesang (IT); Dorjee (graphics and signwriting); and Norbu (fashion). The latter would have his work cut out, as I had tasked him with creating a catwalk fashion show.

Dawa, the event manager, was in his element, rushing around, holding meetings to organise the running order and how the stage, lighting and seating would be set up. I didn't imagine everything would run to plan; orchestrating any event in India was always unpredictable.

'Just remember, India runs on "Indian Standard Time",' my friend Jan told me when I called for our weekly chat. 'Don't expect things to happen on schedule. They will eventually, but not in the way you planned.'

'I know, Jan,' I wailed. 'But we have so little time and so much to do!'

'It doesn't help to get upset or frustrated, Linda,' she said complacently. 'India works in its own special way and there's absolutely nothing you can do about it.'

Standing in the playground in the midday sun on the day of the event, I thought of Jan's words. The stage was still being built. I wanted to stomp around cracking my whip, but when the chai wallah arrived to announce a tea break I decided to let it go. Everyone downed tools and took out their steel tiffin boxes. I sat down with Sonam, my Tibetan guide, general fixer and fast friend, and the workers. They had been doing a sterling job and I didn't want to spoil the day by shouting at everyone. I just had to trust it would all come together.

As the chai wallah poured my tea, he asked a flood of questions: 'Are you married, madam? How much money do you make? Do you sleep with your boyfriend?'

This last comment gained him a slap from Sonam. 'That's enough, my friend,' he said. 'Back to work.' We all fell about laughing.

HRH was due to arrive at 1 pm, and with only an hour to go we still had a lot to do. There were still a few nails to be banged in on the wooden stage, the red carpet had to be laid and water splashed on the dusty trees. Most important, I needed to light the incense sticks we had placed in buckets behind the Prince's chair. I was worried that the wafts of sewage coming from the nearby river might make him retch.

The clock was ticking and I realised that Norbu still had not arrived with my outfit. I had lost my hairbrush in the melee and had the sickening thought that I might have to welcome the Prince of Wales in my dirty black trousers, looking like I had walked through a hedge.

'Linda, time to get changed,' Sonam emerged looking handsome in his dark black Tibetan *chuba* and white silk shirt. 'Your dress has arrived.'

I looked around wildly, taking in all the things that still needed to be done. 'Can you light the incense,' I bleated at him. 'There's still so much to be done.'

'Yes. Go, go, go!'

Norbu had done me proud. I threw on the dress and it fitted perfectly. It was a wraparound *chuba* made of peacock-blue silk that shimmered all the way to the floor. Around the neckline was intricate and sparkly embroidery in contrasting shades of blue. Norbu had chosen a pair of beautiful Rajasthan slippers and a turquoise necklace to match. I could have wept.

Shame there isn't time for a shower, I thought to myself, running my fingers through my hair as I dashed off to the transformed playground.

I was about to clear away the tea cups that had been left lying around when my mobile rang.

'Hi Linda, Eric here. We're running a bit early. Can we bring the Prince now?'

'Now?' I squeaked.

I looked at the men still laying the red flooring. 'Please,' I begged. 'Can you take one more trip around the block? *Please...*'

I waited on the roadside outside the gates of the school for the Prince and entourage to arrive. My phone rang again. This time it was one of the Scotland Yard officers.

'Two minutes and the Prince will be arriving,' he said. 'Are you in position?'

Prince Charles, wearing a double-breasted navy pinstripe suit with a Remembrance Day poppy in his lapel, stepped out of the British High Commissioner's car into the heat and noise and chaos of a three-lane highway. He looked totally at ease.

I had rehearsed my curtsy and welcoming words: 'Your Royal Highness, thank you for coming,' but when the moment came, I opened my mouth ... and nothing came out. I gaped like a fish.

The Prince beamed at me. 'What a delight to be here. Thank you for inviting me.'

A moment later my wits returned and I was able to chat with the Prince as we entered the gates. Once inside, he moved from one entrepreneur to the next, asking questions and looking thoroughly engaged. I could tell he was enjoying himself. He stopped at Norbu's display, particularly taken with the unusual design on Norbu's shoulder bags, made of layer upon layer of silk. He showed them to his private secretary.

'These will make lovely presents,' he said. 'Well done. Stunning!'

Norbu beamed with pride. He had been working around the clock, not only on the clothes and accessories for his stand, but also on my dress and the outfits for the catwalk models. Five ultra-shy Tibetan office girls had been taught by Dawa how to move along the stage to music. It hadn't been an easy job. I had watched him earlier in the day calling out, 'Lift your heads! Stop looking at your toes! The Prince wants to see your beautiful smiles!' His tutelage had not been in vain. Now the models were smiling for all they were worth as they sashayed down the catwalk, and I could tell the Prince was charmed.

As a grand finale we had laid on something very special. I had had to keep my surprise a secret. I had asked Miss Tibet to come to the show. The Chinese had long exerted pressure on governments and organisers to remove Miss Tibet from any international pageants or competitions. I wasn't going to let that happen. We wanted to make a statement, and what better way than to invite Miss India and Miss Tibet to share in the event? Now, as they walked along the catwalk, arm in arm like sisters, we all held our breath, mesmerised by their beauty and grace. They curtseyed to the Prince and he smiled. Later he stood to have his photo taken with the pair. The Tibetans cheered and the press went mad, camera bulbs popping furiously. The moment was captured forever in *Hello* magazine.

Little did I know that this unexpected visit from the Prince would play such a pivotal part of my career. I shared with him my passion for engaging business leaders in my humanitarian projects. He agreed that the private sector was the most underused resource in development work but he quickly added, 'When they start to offer you money, a nice big cheque, leave it on the table. Money is always needed but the real jewel is them, their business acumen, their entrepreneurial skills, their innovation, their creativity, heart, passion and soul. Money is for a moment. The person is for a lifetime.'

Imagine, I thought, *engaging the world's brightest business minds, applying their entrepreneurial skills, passion and creativity to uplift challenged communities sustainably while at the same time transforming their company, their people and their world.* I have. Yes. I believe. *The world needs to stop being charitable and start being capable.*

For many years it had become increasingly obvious that charities were struggling to be effective, with too much red tape, conflict of interest and misdirected funding. The social problems were continuing to grow. What we needed to do was to change the players, change the model and change the approach. Turn the world's brightest minds to the world's biggest problems. Turn to the stars of industry to figure things out and bring their best ideas to the frontline. Stop throwing out cash and start throwing our weight behind real change, one village at a time if need be. My heart and soul were on fire.

The Prince of Wales spent hours in the sweltering heat talking to each of our young Tibetan entrepreneurs. At one point a young Tibetan approached him, offering tea. We had been told he would not be able to accept any food or drink, but he accepted the cup and drank. His interest and concern were evident in every conversation. The Prince finally took his leave long after his allotted departure time. The inspiration and encouragement he gave the group was priceless, and for me a seed had been planted that was to grow into a far-reaching oak tree.

Leadership lesson #8

Most leaders are great talkers but not such great listeners. Active listening is a top leadership skill. Being alert and attentive can pay unimaginable dividends that can change the course of your life. If we learn to listen in a focused manner, without being distracted by the chatter of our own needs, preoccupations and prejudices, we are able to connect more fully, and resolve conflicts and problems more empathically and effectively. Listening and connecting bring gems to light.

Active listening is not easy. Our 'monkey mind' is always busy jumping forward and backward, twisting this way and that. Observe yourself. Do you jump in on a pause and finish the speaker's sentence for them? Do you have your opinion already wrapped up? Be aware: these are signs that you are not fully listening.

***

As a good listener, you will make continuous eye contact. You will constantly check your own understanding against what you are learning from the speaker.

- How well do you listen to others and learn from them?
- Are you really open to what they are saying or are you pretending?
- What do they mean, what are they feeling, and what's at stake?

Do you say no more easily than you say yes?

9

Jump in

How the Boxing Day Tsunami taught me how to start before I'm ready

When a single event is so traumatic that our hearts are wrung by the sheer horror of it, we discover that for the rest of our lives we remember exactly where we were and what we were doing when we heard the news. It was like that when Princess Diana died and when the Twin Towers fell. So it was when on Boxing Day, 2004, at a time when millions were getting ready to eat turkey leftovers with their families, the whole world heard of the deadly blow delivered by the Asian Tsunami. The scale of it was almost unimaginable: waves up to 100 feet high had killed more than 230 000 people in 14 countries, devastating countless coastal communities. It was one of the deadliest natural disasters in recorded history.

At the time, I was in Uzbekistan. It was the end of a tough year and an unforgiving winter. Sitting in my room, late in the evening, I switched on my laptop. When I scanned the news headlines I was brought bolt upright with shock. It was the first time I had ever encountered the word 'tsunami'. I flicked quickly from site to site, feeling a sense of mounting horror. It was clear that, with millions left without food or shelter, the race was on to save lives.

I grabbed my coat and dashed out into the thick snow to look for my closest friend, Habib. It seemed that no one on the streets of Tashkent had yet heard the news. Life continued as normal. A stocky street seller, proudly displaying her knee-length beige pop socks, shouted to me, 'Come and eat. It's delicious!' Normally I would have been tempted to buy a bowl of *plov*, the national dish of lamb, onions and carrots, but today I couldn't stop. A group of old men in woven *tubeteika* caps, drinking industrial-strength vodka, called out their greeting, '*Na sdarovie!*', blithely unaware of the news that was rocking the world.

Habib was at his usual spot, entertaining businessmen in the local restaurant. He was always a generous host and the table was laden with food, pots of black tea and a mind-numbing variety of empty vodka bottles.

'Have you seen the news, Habib?' I screeched over the top of the high-pitched Uzbek lute music. 'I have to go there!'

'What did you say?' Habib cupped his ear, then held up a hand. 'Hold on a minute.'

I had to wait while the waiter performed the usual lengthy tea ritual, pouring tea into a cup from the teapot, then pouring it back again, three times. I usually enjoyed these ancient traditions. Tonight, though, I was breathless with impatience.

'There's been a terrible disaster. I need to talk.'

'Give me 30 minutes and I will get rid of these guys. Meet you at your apartment.'

The men looked quite drunk, so I guessed it wouldn't be long before the meeting was brought to an inevitable close. I dashed back to my room. Where to start? Remembering that a great friend of mine was in Colombo working for the Red Cross, I quickly shot her an email offering my help.

She replied almost immediately. 'Linda, it's a mess here. Aid has started to arrive but much of it is being impounded by the Sri Lankan government. It's just sitting on the tarmac. I wouldn't advise you to come. You'd likely get impounded too.'

I sat back in my chair and paused to think. I felt myself in the grip of an utterly unstoppable drive to *act*. I decided not to contact family or friends. I could hear their responses: 'You can't just pitch up. It's a full-blown disaster area. It'll be chaotic. You don't know anyone there. I doubt you will even be allowed in.'

I called Thai Airways. 'I need a one-way ticket, Tashkent–Bangkok, please. Is there any availability for tomorrow?'

The woman on the phone gave a disbelieving laugh. 'The planes are flying empty. Only three seats sold. Who would want to holiday there now?'

When I told Habib I had bought the ticket he was furious. 'You are one crazy woman! Let the army sort out the chaos. If you really must go, wait at least until they've cleaned up a little.'

He looked at me, then sighed, knowing he was wasting his words. 'Okay. I will book the taxi. And then we'll crack open some bottles. We can't let you go without a bloody good send-off.' Then he wrapped me in his arms in a great big bear hug.

That evening—full of merriment and tears, glasses raised in endless toasts—marked the end of my project in Uzbekistan. A new door had suddenly opened and I needed to walk through it. I was compelled to enter the unexplored room, even though I knew it would be full of horrors, and the only way I could do it was to keep my eyes closed. *Don't think too much. Just go.*

The next day I staggered onto the plane feeling completely numb. The combination of champagne and vodka had done a good job at anaesthetising my brain. Chilled and hungover, I pulled my thick winter coat tightly around me. With that and my fur-lined boots I knew that I would make a strange sight when I arrived in Bangkok. I hadn't been to Thailand for more than twenty years, but my strongest memory was of the intense heat and humidity.

With all the frantic activity before my departure, I'd had no time to research the facts. I had no idea of the geography of the tsunami-hit areas. Once on the plane I flicked through the headlines of the *Bangkok Post* to locate the worst-hit areas, then turned to the map page of the inflight magazine. It seemed that in Thailand the tsunami had caused the most damage at Phi Phi Island and Khao Lak. To reach them I would have to take a domestic flight from Bangkok to Phuket. *How bad can it be?* I thought to myself as I stretched out across four empty seats. *I'll be fine.* Then the alcohol took over and I was dead to the world.

***

My career as an aid worker has never been a conventional one. I prefer to work as an independent consultant, contracted but not employed directly by any organisation. This gives me lots of freedom to find projects, write my own script, fulfil a task and deliver with the aim of making myself redundant. It also means I can take my own initiative, research issues, assess situations, and propose effective and sustainable solutions. Most importantly for me, it enables me to take my own risks.

My mission in Thailand was entirely unplanned—very much a case of 'leap and the net will appear'. I didn't know what I was getting myself into, nor did I have any idea how long I would be involved with this particular project. All I knew was that I had to go.

Unlike the eerily empty plane I had boarded in Tashkent, the domestic flight from Bangkok to Phuket was full. Many nationalities were represented on that plane: distraught relatives, diplomats, and rescue service men and women in fluorescent jackets bearing the name of their organisation. My 'doubt gremlins' were having a field day: *They won't even allow you off the plane. Do you have an official badge? Look at you, in winter coat and boots. It's 30 degrees in the shade out there!*

I was sweating when I left the plane. I knew I didn't look anything like an aid worker—more like an ignorant tourist from Outer Siberia. I decided to flash my UK drivers licence at officials if they questioned me. I collected my case and strode purposefully past the chaotic groups of police and army personnel. As I exited the air-conditioned building, I gasped for breath. It was like walking into a wall of heat, stifling and fierce.

'*Sawadee ka*. Welcome to Thailand.' The taxi driver brought his palms together in a *wai*, a Thai greeting to show respect, lowering his head as he did so. 'Where do you want to go, miss?'

He opened the door and I jumped in. 'Khao Lak, please,' I said quietly. My driver turned around in his seat and stared at me.

'You do not want to go there. Not good place to visit. Not now.' His face was concerned, presuming I was an ignorant tourist.

'Please just take me there,' I repeated, not meeting his eyes.

'I can't, miss. The police tell us only army or rescue workers.'

'I am with the forensic team,' I said. 'My colleagues are already there. I'd be grateful if you could help me to find them. Please.'

A second's pause, then the driver drew out of the airport, heading north in silence. I looked for signs of the disaster but saw none. Tall palm trees lined the streets, and with the clear blue sky and brilliant sunshine it felt like just another day in a tourist resort. Then we slowed to a halt behind a long line of traffic.

'What's happening?'

'Army checkpoint.'

'What are they looking for?' I asked.

'Journalists, disaster tourists,' he said. 'Thieves. Men steal children from the camp. Bad things happening.'

'I really must get through. Is there a side road we can use?'

My plea must have moved him to help. He drew out of the long line of cars and slowly edged past them, one by one. The passengers were a mixed bunch, but I could see that many had cameras. When we reached the front of the line, armed police were waiting next to high rolls of barbed wire. My driver got out of the car and strolled over to them. They spoke for a while, and though I understood none of the words their body language was obvious. It was a 'no', I was sure of it.

Damn, I thought, closing my eyes.

Then … laughter. Two soldiers and my driver were peering at me through the window, grinning. My comically overdressed appearance must have reassured them I was no disaster tourist.

As we drove on the scenery changed dramatically. It began to look like a nuclear bomb had exploded, destroying everything in its path. The land was scarred, flattened, wiped clean.

We reached the top of the hill and parked. We both got out of the car and stood in silence, looking down on the sweeping bay of Khao Lak. The sight was so ghastly my brain simply could not process it. I couldn't seem to focus on anything. A surreal jumble of floating trees, household equipment, upturned cars, suitcases, pillows, bits of houses. I walked to the edge of the cliff and looked over, and wished I hadn't. The sea was full of dead bodies caught up in the debris washed up on the beach, limbs tangled and trapped in the branches of uprooted trees. The water was coated with oil. Several abandoned boats and a passenger barge drifted aimlessly. A few boats under power nudged cautiously through the debris.

I walked back from the cliff edge and sat down hard. My heart was racing. I could feel the sweat trickling down my back and my mouth was so dry my tongue felt enormous. It wasn't just the sight of all that destruction that shocked me. It was the smell. The putrid smell of decomposing bodies was all-pervasive, so bad it made me heave.

My senses were on overload and I felt I was going to faint. Sticking my head between my knees, I pinched myself hard. *I don't think I can do this … it's too much.*

As a nurse I had encountered death fairly regularly, tending to the victims of horrific road traffic accidents and attempted suicides. But this was different. The scale of death, the sheer enormity of it, made me want to turn tail and run. I vomited.

My mind raced and I was catapulted back to my days as a young student nurse. There was matron in her starched white apron; she looked at me sternly and said, 'It's not about you, nurse. You are here to serve, to contribute, to make a difference. *It's not about you.*'

Her clear, calm command brought me sharply back to my senses and to my purpose. I changed my focus to taking some practical action. 'Do you have some water?' I asked the driver. I took a big gulp. Splashed some on my wrists and the back of my neck.

The next thing I knew someone was massaging my shoulders, the touch gentle and reassuring. I turned to see it was a Buddhist nun, dressed in grey cotton. I remained motionless and accepting, my body grateful.

'We are from the north,' said her companion, another nun. 'We have come to help in any way we can.'

It was then I saw that a few small pick-up trucks had stopped near our car. Dozens of men and women, all dressed in the same loose grey cotton trousers and tunics, were setting up camp. They moved about silently, hardly speaking. Seeing them in action was like watching angels on Earth. Every movement they made seemed to speak of unconditional love and compassion.

I got up and brushed down my clothes, my strength restored. I was here to work. I asked the driver to turn the air conditioning up as high as possible. I had a lot to do.

We drove slowly down the hill towards the beach. The scene might have been out of a disaster movie. The wave had left a terrible trail of destruction. Cars had been thrown on top of buildings, where some rested on their roofs, as if a giant had picked them up and hurled them like so many child's dinky toys. We drove past resorts crumpled like crushed matchboxes. Boats had been hurled into the sky, parking meters bent to the ground. A tangled mess of debris. Miles and miles of it. Buses and boats blocked the streets. Electrical power poles were down. Broken glass everywhere.

I could not take it all in. It was like a war zone. A pick-up truck drove by. As it passed us the tarpaulin flapped up in the wind and I caught a glimpse of a pile of bodies, legs hanging out of the back. Inland, lakes had formed, choked with chairs, palm fronds and other debris.

It was impossible to imagine the savage power of the tsunami. I supposed that with all that stuff flying around with such force and with live power lines in the water, if you weren't crushed or sliced to death you might be electrocuted. A living nightmare.

It was beginning to get dark. 'Where are you sleeping tonight, miss?' the driver asked.

'I don't know.'

'Miss, no hotels…all washed away,' my driver said. He looked uncomfortable, on edge. 'I have to go home now. Too many ghosts.'

'You can feel them?'

'They fill my car. I stop at the temple and put them out before I go home. But my mother unhappy. She says she smells them on me.'

Listening to him, thinking of the lost souls clamouring for attention, I felt goosebumps all over.

'Where have the survivors settled?' I asked, changing the subject.

'The camp is at Ban Nam Khem, 35 kilometres north of Khao Lak,' he said. 'The town is gone. Three waves. Nothing left.'

'How many in the camp?' I asked.

'About five thousand,' he said. 'Maybe…four hundred children. Many orphans.'

I lapsed back into silence. My driver turned to look at me, suddenly protective.

'Come back with me, miss. You can't stay there. No water. No electricity. Too many ghosts.'

But my mind was already made up. The camp was exactly where I needed to be—ghosts and all. 'Don't worry, I'll be fine,' I said briskly. 'You need to get going. Please can you drop me at the camp. Thanks, but I can manage perfectly now.'

A little later, he slowed and pointed out two enormous fishing trawlers. They must have been thrown like pebbles, only stopping when they hit the concrete building they rested against.

'Here we are, miss,' he said. 'Easy to find the entrance. Just look for the boats.'

Ahead of us, as far as the eye could see, was a vast sea of canvas. Thousands upon thousands of tents, all colours, pitched without an inch between them. We drove past mountains of old clothes and piles of blankets. I spotted one young woman with blond hair, holding an infant in her arms, and asked my driver to stop. I leapt out of the car and went up to her. She looked exhausted.

'I'm looking for the camp manager,' I said.

She pointed vaguely in the direction of a large army tent.

The driver walked over to a Thai volunteer and spoke quickly to him, then turned to bid me farewell.

'He will show you where to sleep tonight. I must go now.' He wished me luck and climbed back into his taxi.

Leadership lesson #9

Putting off a decision to wait for additional information or for a perfect plan is a recipe for failure. Too often, hesitating in the face of uncertainty allows your competition or circumstances to make the decision for you. Indecisiveness is one of the surest ways to undermine your credibility with your team. Leadership is about accepting and working through uncertainty.

Leaders are always watched. Keeping cool is powerful, even if it's the calm of a swan: serene on the surface but paddling like crazy below. Knowing what you must do and why, and taking action in spite of uncertainty, is great leadership.

***

Overthinking can lead to procrastination and inertia. Detailed analysis and research are not always necessary. Sometimes throwing yourself straight in, with an open mind, will build confidence faster than careful planning.

- How do you react and behave when you experience uncertainty?

- What lies behind your impulse to say *no* rather than *yes*? Is it fear of the unknown?

- What would be a situation in which you would challenge yourself to 'jump in'?

Post tsunami, Thailand

How often do you push the boundaries of your skills and experience?

10
Have fun

How a magician taught me the value of fun and laughter in the midst of grief and death in post-tsunami Thailand

'*Sawadee ka*. What is your name?' I asked the 12-year-old girl at the front of the queue. She limped up to me and stood there, saying nothing. Her face was expressionless. She lifted up her sarong to reveal multiple deep gouges in her legs.

'What happened to you, then?' I asked gently.

The young Thai man who was with her replied, 'We are not sure. She says she was trapped under some trees. Then a car scraped over her. Now she doesn't speak.'

'Are you her brother?' I asked.

'No. We cannot find her family. I found her.' Once I had dressed the girl's wounds, she leaned over and put her arms around my waist. We both found comfort in the hug. During the course of the morning I tended to many other children. Many, like this girl, were mute with grief and shock. I had heard there was a children's tent somewhere in the camp where volunteers were working with the children who had been orphaned or whose families needed support. I decided to set out at lunchtime to find it.

'Tim, I'm going to take a break if that's okay,' I said, wiping my hands. 'I thought I'd go and see what they're doing in the children's tent.'

'Good idea. I've heard they're doing wonderful work there. It's hard to know how to comfort the kids.' He told me he had treated a little boy who had been found clinging to a piece of wood that had lodged in the top of a coconut palm. He had watched his four-year-old sister being swept away.

'What's happened to him now?'

'Well, the real problem is that even if the poor things have survived the wave, the sand and seawater getting into their paranasal sinuses means infection often sets in,' he said. 'He's got it in his lungs and heart. There's not a lot we can do about it. Even with blood transfusions many of them don't survive.'

I heard the children's tent long before I found it. The wonderfully joyous sound of guitars, and the clapping and singing of the volunteers was a welcome relief from the weight of tension and grief that hung over the camp. A jolly, middle-aged woman greeted me with a hug.

'Welcome to children's world.' She introduced herself as Anne and led me into the large canopied area they had set up. 'My group ranges from the youngest survivor here, baby Dee, who's just 25 days old, to this great bunch of teenagers.' She pointed to a group of girls and boys sitting at the knee of a volunteer who was playing guitar.

'Are most of them orphans?' I asked.

'Yes, but not all. Some of them have parents who are so traumatised they're not up to caring for them right now,' she explained. 'They're consumed with worrying about how they're going to survive. They haven't just lost their families. It's their livelihoods too.'

She took my arm and led me to the next tent. 'Come and see what we're doing.' A large blue plastic sheet was spread out on the floor. Every inch of it was covered with large sheets of paper, on which children were working with paintbrushes, completely absorbed. 'We've set up an art therapy program here. Take a look.'

I walked slowly along the rows of children. Their little heads were bent over their work so most of them didn't notice me. I was impressed but also deeply shocked by what I saw, never having encountered traumatised feelings expressed in this way, and on such a scale. It was a great torrent of images, and sometimes words. One little girl had drawn a big wave carrying stick people high into the air, the sea full of smashed boats and floating coconut trees. She had painted a man standing on a rock, arms outstretched, shouting 'Help!' I am used to seeing bright, cheerful children's pictures, with yellow suns and colourful scenes. Here was a different vision. The colours the children had chosen were predominantly dark. I moved closer to see what one teenage girl was writing. She was clutching a pink teddy bear in her left hand, while she wrote in big black letters: 'I hate Tsunami—it took my father, my sister and my uncle. I hate Tsunami.'

'It's extraordinary,' I said to Anne. 'Until now the children I've seen have been barely able to communicate. Here you've got such an outpouring. It's mind-blowing.'

Anne took me to the side of the tent to explain. 'Their psychological recovery will be a very long process. You see, there are multiple layers of loss and grief. Every child has lost many pieces from their everyday framework: loved ones, a teacher, schoolfriends, as well as their homes, their toys, their playgrounds.'

'I imagine the things they experienced will never leave them. The images will remain with them for life.'

'For most of them, yes. But the healing power of the art therapy process really does make a difference, particularly as many of them are still unable to talk about what happened, as you've seen.'

'The colours they're using are so dark.'

'I know, but it's to be expected. They're expressing their nightmares. You know, the rewarding thing about this work is that you get to see lighter colours starting to come in. But it takes time.'

I looked over at the teenagers. 'How is it working with the various age groups? Do they express their hurts differently?'

'They do. We've noticed that the one-to-fives don't eat or sleep well. Most of them are so scared of water that they're refusing to shower. The most demonstrative group seem to be the six-to-tens, who want to be held a lot of the time.'

'And the older ones?' I asked.

'As you might imagine, we're finding the older teens are quick to fire up, hot-tempered—moments of aggression. It doesn't help that they're not sleeping much.'

'What about the younger teens?' I asked.

'They're different again. They tend to internalise their stress. We're getting a lot of complaints about headaches and stomach aches.' Anne sighed. 'The thing is they're not sure if they feel loved any more. They've lost their parents, after all. Some of them clearly don't feel they've got the strength to fight on. It's heartbreaking. And it isn't helping that the adults live in constant fear of another tsunami, and they're passing on this fear to the children.'

For a moment, the jolly, upbeat Anne had vanished and she just looked tired and sad. 'Linda, it's hard for everyone. We don't see many smiles around here.'

Just then a group of nuns, or 'earth angels' as I liked to think of them, appeared from nowhere, like some glorious apparition. One of them called out, 'Ice cream! Who would like some ice cream?' and in a moment they were swallowed up by excited, paint-covered children. Each one came away with a dollop of ice cream in a bread roll.

Something about the fevered creativity in the tent took hold of me. My brain was buzzing with ideas, which came so thick and fast I felt almost giddy with the desire to do something. With every hour I spent in the camp I was getting a clearer picture of how to help. I had been pondering on how I could involve individuals from multinational companies—those with the funds and know-how to help rebuild livelihoods and infrastructure. But my experience in this tent, with these troubled children, had my thoughts racing down entirely different tracks. What could I offer them?

Anne had said it had been vital to move quickly. The longer the children had to wait to get help, the longer they would take to heal. As I walked away from the children's tent I looked back at their paintings fluttering in the warm breeze, hung up to dry on makeshift washing lines. My mind was spinning. What could I do for them, right now?

In the food tent I sat alone, playing with my bowl of noodles, sweat dripping from the end of my nose. I longed for a large glass of water and a shower and vowed never to take water for granted again. My phone bleeped. It was a text message from my parents, checking up on me. Something in that connection triggered an idea...

'Magic!' I shouted, almost causing the small boy sitting next to me to fall off his chair.

I come from a family of magicians. My grandfather, although an amateur, was awe-inspiring. My father carried on the tradition. Now in his seventies, he still wows crowds at friends' parties, sawing my mother in half. As a child I was riveted by Dad's and Granddad's tricks. They taught me some of the simpler ones, which have come in handy over the years. *What does magic do?* I asked myself. The answer was simple. *It brings people joy.* But it's not just that. With magic, language isn't important. And with hundreds of children up and down this battered coast sinking under layers of grief...

I picked up the phone. 'Dad, I need your help. Can you get me the phone number of the president of the International Brotherhood of Magicians?'

I barely had to explain. Dad got it in a millisecond.

'I'll ring you straight back,' he said. 'D'you know, I think this might just work. Good luck, darling.'

In a few minutes I was on the phone to Dan, the president.

'Well, Linda, this one is new to me,' he said cautiously. 'I can see how you'd need doctors and builders...but magicians? It seems a strange idea.' I could almost hear the cogs in his brain clicking as they turned the thought over. *I know it will work. Please see it too.* I was willing him to say yes. 'I'll tell you what I'll do,' he said at last. 'We'll let the members decide. Why don't I announce the idea then we'll wait and see if anyone responds.'

I thanked Dan and put the phone down. *Please, lord, let all those wonderful children's magicians be inspired to come!* I willed them not to think too hard about it, but just to hop on a plane.

And my prayer was answered. Not quite as instantaneously as that, but it happened nonetheless. Within a few weeks, my first volunteer magician had left London for Phuket. Resplendent in the uniform of his profession, with brightly coloured waistcoat and dickie bow, Michael the Magician took the camps by storm. Dripping with sweat, melting daily in the unforgiving swelter, he put on at least three shows a day for three weeks. He performed to crowds of children and adults on the beach, in schools and in the survivor camps. And, whether sea gypsies, widowed old people, orphans or traumatised hotel staff, his audiences delighted in the show.

In no time, Michael was followed everywhere he went, like a pied piper weaving his spell, greeted with shouts of *Abracadabra!* The show needed no words. He told his own magical stories through his actions: producing rabbits, making silk scarves disappear, twisting balloons into animals. He was like a bright butterfly flying around the blackened stumps of a devastated forest.

When he performed his magic show to the children of Ban Nam Khem School, the parents came early and squeezed into the back of the room. The magic seemed to release the tension from their shoulders, smoothing away the lines of worry...for a while at least. The school had taken a particularly severe blow: 150 of its 450 students had been washed away by the wave. Michael's audience was blindsided by grief, having lost so many friends and siblings and children.

'Michael, please come back soon,' I heard the head teacher say. 'Your magic is helping the children find joy in life again. It is the first time I have seen them smile in months. Your magic wand is really working.'

News of the magician's success must have travelled. One morning, I found an email in my inbox:

Dear Linda,

Would a circus be of any use to you and your recovery work? We have a small children's travelling circus, based in UK, and would love to help. We can entertain almost anywhere—we're very mobile. And for small groups we can teach skills. Altogether very therapeutic.

Hope to hear from you soon.

Arabella

Yes! I knew it! Out of one little seed...It's like magic how ideas spread and grow, almost without effort. All you need is some creative thinking and the will to make it happen. It was an inspired idea.

'Send in the clowns!'

In no time at all we had jugglers, stilt-walkers, fire-eaters and Giggles the Clown roaming up and down the survivor camps, spreading a bit of happiness wherever they went. The circus stayed for six weeks and brought a ray of magical sunshine everywhere they set up. They also gave circus skills workshops and trained camp volunteers to perform tricks so their legacy could be continued after they had gone.

One group I had heard about but hadn't worked with were the Morgan people, a community of sea gypsies who, like so many other coastal communities, had been devastated in the tsunami. They had always kept themselves to themselves. Because of this, over the years dark myths had grown up around them, and mothers would warn their children against approaching them. Unsurprisingly, given the fact that they were feared and reviled by other Thais, they hadn't chosen to enter the survivor camps. Instead they had formed their own compound, constructing makeshift shelters from brown hessian strung between bamboo poles and draping them with fishing nets.

I was determined that no group should miss out on the mobile circus experience, so I sought out the sea gypsies' community elders to ask their advice. They accepted our offer with alacrity, giving us the permission we needed to enter their compound.

'Why not?' said one of the old men. 'The children will love it.' He gave a wheezy laugh. 'If the adults don't like it, they will let you know when it is time to leave.'

We had to bribe three reluctant taxi drivers to take us to the sea gypsies' camp. The cars, loaded down with colourful props, which had been crammed into every available space, weaved their way through a complex maze of side streets. The area was coated with a viscous slurry of mud, sand and debris. We made slow progress. Everything and everyone was covered in dirt and the smell of rotting fish was overwhelming.

The village elder greeted us and led us to a small raised area in the middle of the camp, which was to be our stage. I loved how enthusiastic and cheerfully adaptable the circus troupe was. They seemed to think nothing of setting up in such squalid and pitiful surroundings. Immediately, Giggles the Clown, Jill the Juggler and Freddie the Fire-eater set to work, whistling happily, hanging their blue silk backdrop and setting up the sound system. They refused to be spooked by the handful of locals who passed by the stage, every one of them unsmiling and suspicious. We knew the circus group must look a surreal bunch to the sea gypsies, as strange as men from Mars, so it was no surprise that they weren't welcomed with easy familiarity.

'Let's play some music,' said John, once he had donned his Giggles the Clown outfit. 'That might draw them out.'

Soon, the *Pink Panther* theme tune was blaring out and Jill, dressed in an orange afro wig, with yellow oversized sunglasses and a twirling bow tie, got out her juggling balls. She marched to the music, up and down the platform, tapping her big red clown shoes in an exaggerated fashion with each step.

All was still quiet on the street.

Jill then threw three red balls high in the air...then four...then five...then six. Higher and higher they went. She passed them under her legs and behind her back.

Aha! Out of the corner of my eye I saw a few children approaching, dragging their mothers by the hand. Then an old woman carrying a chair plonked herself down in front of the stage. We were on a roll.

Wearing floor-length wizard coats and silly hats, the circus troupe took a bow. The gathering audience was greeted by Freddie who squirted water from a flower in his lapel. Giggles had them captivated when he brought out his magic colouring book. Miming dramatically, he flicked the pages and, on seeing they were blank, stared at them then looked at the audience with the saddest expression, wiping away pretend tears. Suddenly, scratching his head, he had an idea. His eyes lit up, and he ran into the crowd. With his wand he tapped the children's coloured shirts and did the same on the blank book.

By now the children were jumping up and down and screaming with excitement, desperate to take part. Giggles jumped back on stage and dramatically flicked his book again. 'Ta-daa!'

'Woweee!' the audience squealed as each page was revealed, full of brightly coloured pictures. The adults broke into applause and the children cried out for more. The ice was well and truly broken.

There was only one moment when the day nearly came a cropper. It was when Jill the Juggler brought out her magic change bag. She began by walking around the stage and into the audience, proudly showing her big plush red velvet bag. She turned it inside out, showing everyone the sparkly blue lining so they could see it was empty.

Jill had spotted a crowd of teenage fishermen who had gathered at the side of the stage. She went up to them and pointed at a heavy chain one of the lads was wearing around his neck, inviting him to put it into the empty bag. Then, raising her arms like a conductor, she yelled, 'Hocus Pocus!'

'Hocus Pocus!' the crowd replied. So far so good. With a flourish of her wand and another raucous 'Hocus Pocus!' she turned the bag inside-out again. The chain had completely vanished. The small group of teenagers looked decidedly uneasy. The crowd was still laughing and cheering but I was feeling anxious, watching the teenagers become increasingly agitated. A moment later, the biggest of them jumped onto the stage and stood in front of Jill, glaring at her. At this, the crowd was suddenly quiet. Jill may have been alarmed but she didn't show it. With a showman's flourish, she grabbed the magic change bag and trilled, 'Hocus Pocus! Ta-daa!' Out came the chain, glittering in the sunshine, and the crowd, who had been holding their breath, relaxed. Then they clapped even louder than before.

Fred the Fire-eater wrapped up the show as the sun set over the sea.

If only Granddad could see this, I thought to myself.

Leadership lesson #10

Spending too long in your comfort zone dulls the senses, reducing your innovation and creativity, and promoting stagnation and mediocrity. Don't put yourself in a pigeonhole. Push your boundaries. Dare to step up and shine.

People who have fun are less stressed and more engaged, creative and productive. Fun refreshes and rejuvenates us. If we are having fun while we work, our energy levels and motivation are higher and we get more done.

Can a work environment be both fun and effective? Can productivity be increased in a fun, playful workplace? Remember, the opposite of play is not work — it's depression. As a leader, you are responsible for creating an environment that allows your people to give their best effort every day. Great leaders look to build fun environments that motivate, inspire and encourage people to be creative. Think about the environment you would most enjoy working in, then set out to create it.

***

John Shedd said, 'A ship in harbor is safe, but that's not what ships are built for.' Good leadership requires you to step out of your comfort zone and into your learning zone. This is a shift most people aren't prepared to make.

- As a leader, do you need to spend more time in your learning zone? What action will you take to make this happen?

- When was the last time you acted in the face of fear, embracing a new and difficult challenge?

- What can you do more to promote a spirit of constructive play in your organisation?

Why do you think asking for help can make you stronger, rather than weaker?

11

Just ask

How my determination to escalate aid pushed
me through the anxiety of asking for help in
post-tsunami Thailand

There was something worrying me: *me*. The truth is, I simply wasn't
qualified to provide all the business advice these tsunami survivors
needed. And there was no one in the local area I could call in.

One morning, as I doodled on my notepad, hoping for inspiration,
an idea came to me: 'There is an abundance of creative business brains
sitting in Bangkok—company executives who spend their days putting
together solutions to challenging problems.'

Fired up now, I started to make notes, writing quickly. It was clear
to me that many of the survivors of the Asian Tsunami would need to
become entrepreneurs if they were to avoid a bleak future. Although
most had no previous commercial experience, no opportunity to
acquire business skills and no access to loans, they did have a few key
entrepreneurial qualities—among them, courage and determination,
and an overriding hunger to pick themselves back up.

I needed to prepare a compelling business case for the business
community in Bangkok and my possible backer, the Prince of Wales
International Business Leaders Forum (IBLF). I could then work
with the companies in Bangkok to identify opportunities for new

income-generating ventures. Once we had selected those with the most potential, we could develop a simple business strategy for each new entrepreneur.

But I knew something was missing. An idea was hovering at the edge of my mind, niggling at me. There was still one thing I hadn't addressed. Once armed with a new business idea, how would the survivors be able to develop it on their own? They often wouldn't have the necessary skill set or knowledge. Then it came to me: *mentorship!* We needed to build in ongoing support. Partner each entrepreneurial survivor with a business friend who was prepared to share their business skills, to support them, to be there for them when they felt confused or frustrated, when they met an obstacle they didn't know how to overcome. Hold their hand, guiding them in whichever area they needed support, whether it was market expansion, accounting, advertising or customer service. This could mean meeting weekly at the beginning, face to face or by phone, moving to monthly once the entrepreneur became more confident.

'These businesses are always being asked to write a cheque,' I wrote, knowing this would grab their attention. 'Now they're being offered a project they can really sink their teeth into, one that isn't all about money.'

Later, as I pushed the send button on the faded keyboard of my laptop, I closed my eyes and visualised the message winging its way to the Prince of Wales International Business Leaders Forum in London. All I could do now was wait, fingers crossed.

I quickly received an email from the boss himself, Robert Davies, who thought the idea was excellent. He proposed bringing eight of IBLF's business leaders to visit, so they could see for themselves how they could kickstart the whole initiative.

I was overjoyed. Not for the first time, or the last, I sat and cried with thankfulness, reminded again that sometimes all we have to do is ask.

The first group of international and national businessmen and -women from the IBLF, dubbed 'the Tsunami Business Task Force', were tasked with assessing local needs not only in Thailand but also in India and Sri Lanka. The task force included 15 representatives of some of the world's leading businesses, including Accenture, Alcan Inc., Thai Bev, Cadbury Schweppes, Deloitte, ERM Group, Manpower, Nestlé and Standard Chartered. They made Thailand their first stop, arriving in April 2005 and visiting Phuket, Phang Nga and Krabi.

When I was told that the business leaders would be with me for only two days I felt stumped. The distances were vast, and most of our precious time would be wasted in driving from one place to another. I pondered the problem for days, finally deciding that the only way it could work logistically would be to use helicopters. But how on earth was I going to swing that one? I took a deep breath and picked up the phone. I decided to call the Admiral in Charge of Tsunami Relief at the Navy base at Cape Panwa, at the foot of Phuket Island.

Maybe it was crazy to think that the Navy would hand over a couple of helicopters at the request of a *farang* woman, a person of European ancestry, but at the time that thought didn't even enter my head. I had no doubt it was a good idea.

The next day I was received at the Navy base with all the pomp and ceremony that only the military can pull off. Luckily, I always have one nice frock with me, and on this occasion I pulled out all the stops, adding lipstick, perfume and blow-dried hair. The Admiral, who must have been in his fifties, had a formidable presence. He stood to greet me, straight-backed in his immaculate uniform, shoes and buttons gleaming. I glanced down at my pumps, relieved that I had remembered to give them a wipe. He invited me to sit. I started nervously but he was a good listener. Soon I was pouring out my plans and goals, and all the while his eyes never left my own. He asked all the right questions, and once he had the facts he was very decisive.

'Of course they've got to see what's going on firsthand. I think it's a splendid idea.' He scratched his chin. 'Tell you what. I will give you two eight-man helicopters for two days.'

I nearly fell off my chair.

'Let us know where your business leaders are staying and we can pick them up from there—it will save time. And why don't we conclude their visit with a trip to the base here for a presentation of our military strategy for recovery?'

'Thank you so much, sir,' I stuttered, feeling overwhelmed.

'You are very welcome, young lady. Your passion to help the Thai people at the grassroots—at the very heart of our problems—has moved me deeply.'

Later that evening at the café I sat with some of my fellow volunteers, who huddled close, eager to find out how I had got on. I grinned at them and raised my beer glass in a salute.

'I needed helicopters. They had them!' I declared. 'There's never any harm in trying.'

The two days flew by. The business leaders, who were accompanied by the British ambassador, were tireless. Snatched from their comfortable lives, they visited the worst-hit areas, never flinching from the dirt, the heat, the grief and despair. They talked to disabled survivors, orphaned children and fishermen, all the while listening to their stories and needs.

On the second day, I had planned an unusual dinner for the group. It had occurred to me that after any catastrophic disaster the main stakeholders in the recovery process, which always include the government, the military, the media, the charity sector and the business sector, don't always talk to each other. Each is heavily engaged in vital work, racing frantically to meet deadlines and achieve their goals. I had already witnessed overlap in Thailand. It was clear that these groups needed to communicate. I was hoping that my dinner would kickstart that process.

I decided that my dinner guests needed to be from the top of the tree—no middle management or lieutenants, I needed CEOs and admirals. This group, later billed as the 'Disaster Rapid Response Team', comprised leaders from the following groups:

- *the government of Phuket* (responsible for the population and recovery strategy)

- *private sector* (business skills and resources for emergency and livelihood recovery)

- *NGOs* ('strengthen the buffalo to plough the field': generally the ones with the strong local contacts and experience)

- *military* (strategy, manpower and equipment)

- *media* (often first on the scene—the Thai public donated more aid money to the leading TV channel in Thailand than they did via the government because the camera crews were reporting the developing situation, minute by minute, and communicating the immediate needs).

The Governor of Phuket, Udomsak Uswarangkura, thought the dinner was a marvellous idea, as did the head of the main national TV channel, a senior representative of the Red Cross, and *two* admirals. Their presence around the dinner table at the Sheraton Hotel in Phuket that second night ignited the beginnings of a real plan of how best to work together. The information was later used as part of a powerful publication, *Best Intentions, Complex Realities.* Now we had agreed channels of communication I knew that the relief and recovery work would be more effective and sustainable. There would be much less overlap and time wasting.

Watching the large group around the table engaging so energetically was heaven. I sat back in my chair and enjoyed the scene, as the conversation sparked back and forth, taking on a life force of its own. There was no need for small talk that night. At one point the ambassador, who was sitting opposite me, caught my eye and winked, leaning across the table to say, 'You did good, Linda. What an evening!'

Leadership lesson #11

Sometimes the task is beyond our capacity or expertise and we simply don't know how to handle it. We may vaguely ask for help, or blame others, or procrastinate until it becomes an emergency. Asking for help can be tough. Fear of being a burden, fear of admitting we are not in control, fear of owing a favour, fear of appearing weak and, above all, fear of rejection—there are so many reasons why we don't ask for help.

Yet people love to help, although often they don't know how. Each of us has different resources and capabilities. Draw on the power of the team. As a team, the whole is much more powerful than the sum of its parts.

***

Put your ego and fears aside and take the spotlight off you. Asking your team for ideas is a way to show them you trust them, feel confident in their skills and value their advice. Asking for help, insights and opinions from people outside of your inner circle will generate fresh ideas and perspectives on how to solve problems, creating better, stronger results.

- Does your ego stop you from asking for help?
- Are you asking the right person?
- If you ask someone for help, what gift or opportunity are you giving them?

Post tsunami, Thailand

Do you take charge in order to serve or to dominate?

12

Take charge

How sudden danger brought out the lion in me in Pakistan

After our nightmare drive from the terrible floods in northern Sindh province to the capital, Mahdi dropped me at the Karachi airport for a 6 am flight to Islamabad. I called Faisal, my trusty driver, with my arrival time and told him I needed to go straight to the offices of the World Bank.

Faisal had asked me to wait inside the terminal building if I couldn't see him. After a couple of minutes I ventured a peek outside and saw him running towards the airport building, his white *shalwar kameez* billowing out behind him. With increased security around the airport, he hadn't been able to park out front. The Red Mosque siege had been dragging on for weeks, totally disrupting the city, and tensions were high.

'Madam, please hurry,' he said, grabbing my suitcase and striding briskly back towards the main road.

Ahead of us there was a commotion: a small crowd of highly animated men were watching a police forklift truck clearing a car from a restricted area. To my horror, I realised it was ours. Faisal was wide-eyed with panic. The embassy's advice had been clear: *During this volatile time, do not linger in public places*. I knew that every second the danger increased and our chances of a safe exit were ebbing. Without stopping to think, a combination of fear and desperation propelled me forward. I ran towards the policeman who was overseeing the operation.

'Put it down!' I said emphatically, pointing at the car, which was suspended in the air above us.

The man looked at me in disbelief.

'Put it down,' I said again firmly, pointing first at the car then the ground. 'This is my car, and I am late.' I tapped my watch. 'I need to leave now. Right now. Put it down!' My voice was as commanding as a head teacher's.

Out of the corner of my eye I saw Faisal shifting nervously from one foot to the other, sweat beading on his forehead. The policeman was still staring at me, goggle-eyed. He held my gaze a moment longer, then turned, signalling for the forklift driver to lower the car.

'Thank you.' I said sternly, maintaining an air of authority.

We leapt into the car and shot off. My knees were shaking.

On rare occasions the shock factor of playing the bold, assertive foreign woman in Pakistan worked to my advantage. This was certainly one of them.

Leadership lesson #12

There are moments when it is essential to step up, be firm and take control. In times of stress or confusion, when the skills and abilities—perhaps even the values—of those around you appear to be unequal to the task, it is important to have the courage to take charge. Taking charge does not mean asserting your authority in an oppressive way. It means gathering those around you and leading them to a better place.

Maintain excellent relationships. An assertive leader who is respected, admired and liked will find it easier to influence others to take on difficult tasks, where an assertive leader who is not will get only resistance. A leader who serves, who puts the needs of others first, can unleash reciprocal action, purpose and ingenuity.

***

Respected leaders are consistent and fair in the small things as well as the large. They start work at the same time, put in the same hours and take the same lunch breaks as their staff. They are trusted, so when action is needed the team will not question it.

- Are you a selfless leader who puts your people's welfare ahead of your own?

- Do you take the time to communicate clearly and personally?

- Do you allow your people to take a compassionate day as often as you yourself might take one?

Part III

Love

No one cares how much you know, until they know
how much you care.

Theodore Roosevelt

Are you living the life you were born to live, or is it time for change?

13

Purpose and passion

How I lost my sight and found my vision one cold, dark night in England

I had been an adventurous child of adventurous parents. We weren't the sort of family to holiday at the nearest seaside resort each summer like everyone else. We took the car and zigzagged across Europe. My parents were both committed Cub Scout leaders and I worked hard for every badge, out in all weather. I took their mottos very seriously: 'Do a good turn daily' and 'Be prepared'. On our family camping holidays we would sit out under the stars while my dad taught us their names. He would say to us, '*Vive la différence!* The world is just waiting to be explored.'

In the early 1990s I thought I had everything—married with two wonderful children, living in a smart townhouse, enjoying a challenging career in nursing. It all came to an end quite suddenly. After the divorce, to make ends meet I had to leave nursing, a career I adored, and ended up in a dead-end job that ticked all the financial boxes but made me miserable and anxious.

Then, in 1996, came that terrifying, fateful night drive (recounted in the preface), when I suffered sudden, total blindness, which I would later learn was triggered by work stress. And I vowed then that if my sight returned, I would make serious changes to my life. I would fulfil my quest to find out what it was I was born to do. It was my wake-up call.

Back home, and sighted once more, I started to analyse my day-to-day life. Living had stopped being fun a long time ago. I noticed that conversations with family and friends were too often tirades of negativity, complaining and moaning, with rarely a positive word passing my lips. 'The weather is going to be bad today,' a friend would say. 'And it'll be worse tomorrow. We never get good weather,' I would retort, piling on the pain.

I caught myself remembering every last detail of bad news from the TV and radio, eagerly regurgitating it to anyone who would listen. Shocked, I realised I had become a really miserable person. It had to stop. I had heard that real change happens only when you can no longer tolerate where you are. I had reached that point. I swore I was not going back!

I was determined to change my life from negative to positive, and do so as quickly as possible. I called this my Emergency Zen. I committed myself resolutely and passionately to stop bitching, stop complaining and stop worrying. I would purge myself of negative speech and thought. No more negative talk, email or even journal reflections. I quickly understood that whatever I gave energy, attention and focus to would expand. My goal: to live my purpose, to help others, to experience happiness as never before and to become a magnet for love.

I devised a plan of action and stuck to it ruthlessly. My best friends—persistence, commitment and discipline—took my hand as I stumbled along this new, unfamiliar path.

Emergency Zen:
My 7-step program

1. **Turn off the news...now!** Don't read a newspaper or magazine. You need a media-free week, to liberate yourself from that constant drip, drip of bad news and disaster stories. Remember, you attract to your life whatever you give your attention to, whether it is positive or negative.

   Having eliminated the news, fill that space with positive things. A vacant space is just waiting to be filled back up with energy drainers. Think about and select activities, places, people and things that bring a smile to your face. Intentionally incorporate more fun into your life.

2. **You become who you associate with.** Think about the key people you spend time with each week. Are they frustrated, happy? Do they share your values? Do they encourage you when you speak of your goals and dreams? Do you feel drained or brought down after a phone call with any of them? When you're making your life change, you may need to distance yourself from those who don't vibrate in harmony with you.

   Places can also sap your energy. Choose to spend time with nature. Even vary your route to work. Whatever boosts the feel-good factor.

3. **You are what you speak.** Reframing your language will lessen its negative potential. A *problem* becomes a 'challenge'; a *risk* becomes a 'possibility'; a *setback* becomes a 'detour'.

4. **Zip it up.** Speak only when you have something positive and constructive to say. Your friends, family and colleagues will appreciate the change.

(continued)

Emergency Zen:
My 7-step program (*cont'd*)

5. **Expect the best possible outcome.** Accept that even setbacks may have a purpose. HH the Dalai Lama says, 'Remember that not getting what you want is sometimes a wonderful stroke of luck.'

6. **Thank you!** Stop taking things for granted. Make a list of everything you're grateful for. Gratitude is all about recognising what we have and what is going well in our lives, rather than what we haven't got. Thank others, and don't forget to thank yourself.

7. **Be the change.** Intentionally feel the gift of 'paying it forward'. One of our basic human needs is to be useful, to feel needed. Make every day a good deeds day. You will find that helping is addictive.

Ask a 'change buddy' to keep you on track, and don't be surprised by those who might want to sabotage your efforts, who might feel threatened by the change in you. Beware the naysayers, the ones who would prefer you to stay the same. Your negativity 'fast' may annoy a few people, especially any previous moaning buddies. It takes at least two to have a really good moan. You may even lose some 'friends'—I did.

I quickly understood that whatever I gave energy, attention and focus to would expand. My goal: to live my purpose, to help others, to experience happiness as never before and to become a magnet for love.

Back in 1996 I had recognised that my dream—aligned with my skills and passion—was to serve on the humanitarian frontline. I wanted to be a hands-on carer again, but not in safe, sanitised England.

I wanted to help in communities on the edge that had no financial security and no social security to fall back on.

Two years later I sold everything I owned, including house, car, paintings, furniture and books.

Eighteen years on, my possessions still fit into a single suitcase. Yet my life is rich and full of purpose.

Leadership lesson #13

Leaders who live a life of purpose have core beliefs and values that influence their decisions, shape their day-to-day actions, and determine their short- and long-term priorities.

Talented people want to be part of something bigger than themselves. They want to see their ideas and efforts produce something truly significant. People who feel that their work doesn't matter, that they aren't important to the organisation, will quickly become disengaged.

Every individual has gifts and talents that can make a lasting impact. Only a few, however, utilise those gifts and talents and live to their full potential. As a leader, it's your job to uncover employees' strengths, encouraging their development and passion.

***

Think about your team's purpose and why it exists. Consider what you have in common as a team, your common goals and focus, and what others might see as your purpose.

- Do you measure success in business terms or by your own wealth or status?

- Do you have everything but still feel that there is something missing?

- Do you wake up every morning eager to face the day, to build something, to be the change?

Tibetan Plateau

How often do you really dig deep and pay attention to those you lead?

14

Dig deeper

How learning to be tenacious paid off with love in the Atlas Mountains of Morocco

The road from Asni to Imlil meandered along a dried-up river bed. It was a startling, lunar-like landscape. My driver snaked his way through the canyon, under rocky ledges, the air getting distinctly cooler as we climbed. Finally there it was above us: the famous Kasbah du Toubkal, perched on a hilltop framed by the towering High Atlas Mountains. It took my breath away. Hajj Maurice had asked me to lunch and had warned me that the hotel could be accessed only on foot or by mule. He told me to wear sensible shoes and to ask for directions from Imlil, the village tucked into the valley below.

Imlil, it turned out, was no more than a small row of shops and restaurants that served the backpackers who wanted to conquer Mount Toubkal, the highest peak in Morocco. A shopkeeper pointed out the route to me and I climbed for 15 minutes through fragrant apple orchards and walnut groves. When I reached the top, I was panting. The hotel receptionist invited me to sit down (presumably before I collapsed!). While I held my hands over a metal bowl, he poured rosewater over them in a traditional Berber greeting. I was then given a date to eat, and a bowl of milk to dip it into.

Rather than being run by professional expat hoteliers, all the staff of this spectacular hotel in the mountains, including manager

Hajj Maurice, were local Berbers. The far-sighted and generous British owners of the hotel, Mike and Chris McHugo, showed a real dedication to helping the community, energetically raising money for local projects. And they had given Hajj Maurice the responsibility to ensure it was well spent. I was keen to meet the man in whom they, and the local villagers, put so much faith.

'Hajj is expecting you. He said to take you to the terrace,' the man said.

I followed him outside and waited for my host, flicking through a picture book, *The Making of Kundun*. Martin Scorsese had used the hotel as a film set in his movie about the Dalai Lama. I looked down at the valley below and wondered how the hell he had got crew and camera equipment all the way up here.

'Linda! *Bienvenue!*' Hajj gave me a warm handshake. The receptionist stayed with us as translator.

I was amazed to see that Hajj, a man with an enormous reputation locally, was under five feet tall. His heavy grey *djellaba* seemed to swallow him up. Despite his slight frame, there was an aura about him—a suggestion of both power and wisdom. After some small talk I explained that Virgin had asked me to assess the healthcare issues in this isolated area. I asked him what he thought were the key needs.

'There is no phone signal up there.' He pointed towards the mountains. I looked at the paths crisscrossing them like tiny veins, and thought they looked treacherous. 'In an emergency the villagers cannot reach anyone quickly. Their only option is to carry the sick down to a road and call for help from there. Many don't make it that far.'

'What medical staff are there?' I asked.

'We have no doctor. Just one nurse. Hameed. Works in Imlil.' Hameed, it seemed, was responsible for the total medical care of more than 20 000 people. 'Mother and baby care. Vaccinations. Accidents. He does it all.' Hajj explained that there was a high incidence of diabetes in the area. I thought instantly of the copious amounts of sweetened mint tea I had seen drunk. Heart attacks and strokes were equally common.

'And your nearest doctor?'

'We have a small clinic in Asni. There's a doctor there who holds daytime clinics a few times a week. Otherwise it's Tahanaout, which has a small Accident and Emergency department. After that, Marrakesh.'

The conditions at the clinic in Asni were very basic. 'In winter, there's no heating. The mothers have to give birth in the freezing cold.' And they were desperately in need of midwives, as women in this conservative community refused to be tended to by men.

'In Asni clinic alone, there are 620 births a year.'

'How on earth do they cope?'

'It's a bit crazy. With the lack of qualified staff here, most women end up giving birth at the hospital in Marrakesh.'

'But that's a 90-minute drive!'

'A long way if you're in pain,' Hajj agreed. When he suggested I should meet Abderahim, their ambulance driver, I told him that his was the other name I had heard most frequently on people's lips.

Hajj smiled tenderly. 'He's a father of three young boys. Loves his family. Loves his job. Do you know he's never had a day's medical training in his life? All he knows he has learned on the job.'

The more Hajj told me about Abderahim, the more I understood why he was held in such reverence. A man on call 24 hours a day, 365 days a year. And all for less than $45 a week.

'Entirely his choice,' Hajj explained. 'The government doesn't pay him to work those hours. Everyone loves him. He has saved many lives.'

Hearing about Abderahim made my heart swell with gratitude. That there are inspirational role models like him out there reminds you how powerful and selfless the human spirit can be.

Mohammed, the singing muleteer, was waiting to take me down the hill. I bounced along as my mule navigated the rocky ravines, marvelling at the ungainly-looking animal's extraordinary agility. When we got to Asni, Hameed was in his clinic, a long line of patients waiting to see him. I poked my head in.

'Hello, I'm Linda. Hajj sent me.'

'Oh, hi. I hear you're a nurse,' he said. 'Why don't you sit next to me and you'll get a feel for what we're doing here. In 30 minutes we can stop for lunch.'

I sat down. We were in an icy, cave-like room. It didn't look anything like a clinic.

'Please excuse the room,' Hameed said, seeing me look round the room, aghast. 'It's the garage for the ambulance. The clinic room is being repaired. I couldn't close up, as the government recommended, so I've parked the ambulance outside.'

He made good use of the cramped space. Behind a green hospital screen was a bed for examinations. He had rigged up an IV device on the unplastered garage wall. On a desk was a set of baby scales and on the back wall there was a fridge to store the vaccines.

It was obvious that everyone loved Hameed. He listened carefully and tenderly to each patient's problems. If a child was in tears they soon dried up when he spoke to them.

Just before lunch, a man limped in. He had fallen off his bike and there was a large, bloody slash across his knee.

'Looks like we will need to sew this one up,' Hameed said.

I asked him how on earth he managed to keep the place sterile. There was no source of water in the room.

'As best we can,' he said with a grimace. 'We use plenty of this.' He was brandishing a big bottle of bright-orange iodine. 'It kills all known germs!'

Over lunch, Hameed described his work. I could see how overstretched and frustrated he was. He wanted to go on training courses but there was no one to stand in for him at the clinic. He needed more equipment, especially diagnostic items. The government gave them a meagre supply of basic dressings and medicines each month, but once that was gone he had nothing until there was a new delivery. It was all inadequate, unpredictable and unreliable. What was heartening, though, was how much Hameed loved his job in spite of the problems.

'Can I meet Abderahim today?' I asked, crossing my fingers.

'He was delivering a baby at three this morning,' he said, pulling out his phone. 'I'll give his wife a call and see if he's up yet. He sleeps whenever he can.'

He spoke briefly on his mobile, then said, 'You're in luck. He'll meet us at the ambulance.'

When we arrived, Abderahim was cleaning the headlights of the ambulance. Hameed called out to him. He looked up and beamed at his friend. Hameed, speaking in Berber, told him about my project. Abderahim turned to me, and I saw how tired he looked, older than his years. He told me that he spoke a little French, but no English. I was used to that by now and my French was becoming a little more fluent every day.

'How long have you been working the ambulance?' I asked.

'Ten years. I delivered a beautiful baby boy in the back last night. We tried to get the mother to the clinic in time but the baby came so quickly.'

Abderahim opened the ambulance door. 'We don't have much equipment.'

There was only a stretcher bed and a stretcher chair, one blanket and a pillow. A small first aid cabinet was on the wall but it was virtually empty. There seemed to be only one bandage inside.

Hameed patted his friend's back. 'Never a day's formal training and he saves lives every week. Whenever he can, he sits in at the clinic, listening and learning,' he said. 'He must just be a natural physician.'

My survey kept me in the mountains for a few weeks. There was something about Hameed that kept niggling at me, something he was not saying. He looked chronically tired and his nurse's white coat was rarely remotely white. For weeks I had been asking to visit his home, but always something happened: an unexpected patient would turn up, the moment was gone and the visit postponed.

With two weeks to go before I was due to leave I was determined to solve the mystery. I felt certain that his home would give me some clues. 'I still haven't seen where you live, Hameed.' As he began to once more redirect the conversation to the patients he could not miss the determination written clearly on my face.

His face forlorn, Hameed stood up, resigned to do as I asked. He led me behind the clinic, down an overgrown path and through a small wooden doorframe with no door.

'This is where I live,' Hameed whispered, his head and shoulders drooping in shame. I was stunned. The room was the size of a dog's kennel. I could feel the wind whipping through the broken roof. 'Where do you sleep? Where do you wash? How can you cook?' The questions fell from my mouth in a flood of anger.

A metal hospital bed stood in one corner, no mattress. There were no chairs, nowhere to wash, no toilet.

'You must freeze in here when the snow falls and boil when the summer comes!' I tried to keep calm. 'This is not acceptable, Hameed. You care for 20 000 patients. And you live like this!' My voice reached a crescendo.

'I am okay, Linda. Really, please don't worry,' Hameed said in his gentle, accepting way.

Fuelled by anger and a tight timeline I reached out to all my contacts and friends at Virgin. I refused to leave Morocco until Hameed had a home, somewhere he could sleep, wash and rest after all his dedicated hard work. Everyone rallied around. The roof was fixed, a washroom was put in, a carpet was laid, chairs arrived, along with a bed complete with mattress, sheets and duvet.

After many smiles and hugs, I left Imlil with a spring in my step. Hameed had his place.

A year later I returned to visit. Eager to see my old friend, I knocked on the door of his little home. A beautiful lady opened the door, Hameed close behind. 'Linda, may I introduce you to my wife, Ayesha.' He was beaming from ear to ear. 'I am teaching her to help me in the clinic. She is a wonderful wife.'

A warm glow fell over us all.

The following year I returned for my now annual visit. To my surprise and delight, cooing away in her cot was a beautiful baby girl. 'Linda, please do come and meet Amina.' I could not stop my tears of joy.

Hameed took me to one side and sat me down. 'Thank you for *seeing* me, thank you for not giving up. Because of your determination to find out about me, I now have a wife and baby. With my broken house I was unable to ask for a wife. I would have been alone my whole life. Now my life is complete.'

Leadership lesson #14

Observation is a skill all leaders should work on. When we see someone or something every day we develop blind spots. We lose our 'fresh eyes'. When leaders talk less, listen more and intentionally watch closely what is going on around them, they begin to discern subtle yet vital details that enable them to lead more effectively.

We gain invaluable insights when we move into observation mode. It also helps us to see the bigger picture. We see patterns, trends, synchronicities and dissonances; we read and understand non-verbal cues such as body language and the interplay between team members; we sense mood and energy levels in meetings; we become aware of what language lights our people up—and conversely what leaves them flat.

***

Be curious. Observe others carefully, especially the quiet ones. Pay attention to the givers. Dig deeper. Be tenacious. Keep asking questions if you feel you are not getting the real answer.

- How often do you sit in a meeting purely to observe?

- What is your team not saying? What non-verbal cues are you picking up?

- Who are the quietest, and why?

Ambulance team, Atlas Mountains, Morocco

Do you invest routinely in your own health and welfare, no matter how busy your life?

15

Take care of yourself

How I was stopped in my tracks in
Delhi—pampering or bust!

In the Tibetan refugee camps I listened to many youngsters venting their
frustration at not being able to find jobs. As aliens, they did not have the
right to seek work in the Indian civil service and they couldn't see how
they would be able to penetrate the Indian job market. I thought about
what might be done and arranged a meeting with Colonel Singh from
the Mysore Indian Chamber of Commerce. Together we discussed the
possibility of arranging a job fair. If businesses that were open to hiring
Tibetans could be persuaded to attend, then the fair might create a
useful bridge. The colonel agreed that there was a need for new channels
to improve the Tibetans' job prospects. Like many Indians I had spoken
to, he had nothing but good will towards the Tibetans. He knew
them to be honest and hardworking. The problem was that he never
saw them. He could see the need for new initiatives.

Samdhong Rinpoche, a Buddhist monk who was also the Prime
Minister of the Tibetan government-in-exile based in Dharamsala,
had received my field report, which suggested setting up formal links
with Indian business groups who were receptive to hiring Tibetans. He
discussed it with his teams to work out how this would be sustainable

across India, linking to each of the refugee camps. In the meantime, I continued to talk to local businesses. One of the most important links came about quite by chance. On my frequent taxi rides across Delhi, a poster kept catching my eye. It featured the famous face of Shahnaz Husain, with her enormous mane of hennaed hair and the equally impressive diamond stud in her nose. Curious to find out more about her, I did some research.

Shahnaz's story was legend. The founder of Shahnaz Herbals, an ayurvedic range of beauty products and a chain of salons, she had managed to convert a teenage passion into a multimillion-dollar beauty industry with an empire that stretched from Seoul to Dubai. Shahnaz is an Iranian Muslim who moved to India at the age of 13, was engaged at 14 and a mother at 16. She built up her business until it was the largest organisation of its kind in the world, with hundreds of franchise clinics worldwide and beauty and health care formulations.

As I trawled through Shahnaz Herbal's website, something caught my eye. Shahnaz had received the 'World's Greatest Entrepreneur Award' from *Success* magazine in the United States, the first woman in 107 years to do so. I gave her a call.

When my Tibetan friend Sonam heard that she had invited me to her house for a meeting he was impressed. 'She's like royalty here,' he said. 'People think of her as their princess. They love her.'

'Well, that's what your cause needs,' I replied. 'If she likes the project she'll have the power to move it along. That's what we need—entrepreneurial people with spirit.'

What I couldn't have foreseen was that not only did they take up the Tibetan youth cause and run with it long after many other businesses and agencies had dropped out, but Shahnaz and her daughter Nelofar would become two of my greatest friends and supporters.

I was met at her house by a friendly army of security guards and servants, and led to a palatial sitting room with deep-piled white carpets, white walls and furniture, and flowers everywhere. It looked like someone had designed a movie set of heaven. Shahnaz, an imposing figure in a floor-length leopard-print Louis Vuitton robe, made a magnificent entrance. She must have been six foot in her heels. Her personal photographer and videographer followed in her wake.

'Do sit down, Linda,' she said. 'You look exhausted.'

I did as instructed and almost disappeared in her pillowy sofa. I was prepared to pitch my project to Shahnaz, but she was so well briefed that I let her do the talking.

'I know all about what you are trying to do,' she said. 'I want you to meet my daughter Nelofar. She's the one leading our community development work.' And then, before I could say anything, she continued: 'I know exactly how we can help you. But first I want you to do something for me.'

'Of course. What would you like me to do?'

'Take a day off,' Shahnaz said. 'You look very tired.' Before I could protest, she had picked up the phone and booked me a full round of treatments at her spa downstairs.

'You, my dear, need pampering,' she said. And she was off, telling me about everything that would be done to my body, including an oxygen facial. Having only recently returned from Mainpat, where there had been no running water and I had to wash using a bucket, I was speechless.

Shahnaz read my face and hers scrunched up in displeasure. 'You must never neglect your femininity.'

I had to concede that pampering myself hadn't exactly been high on my list of priorities, and she had a point—I had got run down. I decided to go with the flow and found myself asking her how she made her hair look so gloriously lustrous. It seemed heroic quantities of eggs, lemon juice, olive oil, henna, ground coffee beans and tea were involved. *Goodness,* I thought. *It was like listening to a chef with an equal measure of passion and obsession.*

'You see, Linda,' she said, 'I take care of myself, and so should you. Now off you go. No more talk.'

As I said goodbye to Shahnaz, I felt a sudden urge to cry. It had been a while since I had last been cared for. In the life I had embraced I had chosen to look after other people's needs, but in the process had forgotten to care for myself. Shahnaz had grasped my situation in a millisecond.

The next week I met with Nelofar, an equally stunning woman with the same extraordinary hair as her mother's. We got on immediately. She asked me how much I wanted her to donate.

'Well actually, nothing,' I said.

She looked surprised. It wasn't often that someone turned down the offer of money.

'What I was hoping,' I explained, 'is that you would be prepared to offer an apprenticeship in one of your beauty salons to a girl from one of the Tibetan camps.'

I explained that our program was all about offering empowerment and creating independence in these young people. Nelofar listened carefully while I outlined my ideas, nodding thoughtfully, never once interrupting.

'I know they can be very timid, but that will not matter,' she said thoughtfully. 'The important thing is that Tibetans have a reputation for being caring. And that is just what we need in the beauty business.'

She told me what the training would entail and I jotted down the details. 'It will take six months,' she said. 'And will cover hairdressing, skincare, haircare, manicure, pedicure, bridal make-up, waxing, threading, and health and wellness.'

I was excited. The girl I had in mind, Dolma, would be ecstatic when she heard what was in store for her.

'Bring her to my Khan Market salon on Monday,' Nelofar said. 'I'll speak to my salon manager right now.'

I rushed off to break the news to Dolma, but she wasn't so much ecstatic as terrified.

'I don't think I can do it,' she stammered. 'It is the top salon in India. They are all Indian.'

We talked it through. I promised to come with Dolma and introduce her to the staff, and I would pop in regularly to check she was okay.

The following Monday, Nelofar herself was at the salon to greet us. She welcomed Dolma warmly and her Indian staff followed her lead. I sat in the corner of the salon chatting to Nelofar as Dolma assisted in her first cut and blow dry, sweeping the floor, folding the towels, and bringing the clients coffee.

'She will be fine,' said Nelofar. 'I've given her to my best manager. I'm in here most days. I'll see she's okay.'

I thanked Nelofar and left the salon feeling reassured. I had arranged to meet Dolma regularly in the camp so we could talk over any problems she had. At our initial catch-up she spoke tentatively at first, explaining that the travelling was tiring and the local buses were crowded. It wasn't long, though, before her enthusiasm took over, and she described her work with pride.

'A client asked specially if I could do her manicure and pedicure,' she said. 'They tell me that I am good at varnishing.'

'That's wonderful,' I said. 'And how are you getting along with the other girls in the salon?'

'They like me, I think,' she said. 'They help me if I don't know how to do something.'

Excellent, I thought.

Nelofar called me shortly before Dolma's six-month training was due to finish.

'Let's meet up,' she said. 'It's time to celebrate.'

Nelofar was very pleased with Dolma's performance. 'We'll miss her, and so will the clients. The girl's a natural entrepreneur!' She pronounced her all set to return to her mountain village to start up her own business.

'Do you think she's ready for that?' I asked.

'Don't worry. We'll keep in touch with her and keep her training updated,' she said. 'Now it's time for you bring another Tibetan girl to us. We've got work to do!'

True to her word, Nelofar supervised the 'hand up' of one Tibetan girl after another. She wouldn't take any thanks for her generosity. Instead, she thanked me.

Smiling, she put her hand on my arm. 'As one of my favourite Chinese verses says, a little fragrance always clings to the hand that gives you roses.'

Leadership lesson #15

Burnout, sometimes called 'overachiever syndrome', costs businesses and individuals dearly. More importantly, it costs lives. Pride pushes you to think you can handle anything. Fear keeps you from telling anyone you can't. And the stigma attached to anxiety and depression makes it impossible for many leaders to talk about it.

One casualty for leaders who feel they are not fulfilling purpose and passion is their heart: it grows dull and may even die. You just don't *feel* what you used to. Your happiness is gone.

Each of us needs mental, emotional and physical care. If you are not rested and healthy, you will not get where you want to go.

***

Set up systems to help monitor and manage your stress. For example, arrange with a friend or colleague to alert each other when signs of stress show. Take a day off. Shut off your phone. Cancel some meetings. Take a vacation. You show others how to treat you by the way you treat yourself. Nurture, nourish and take care of yourself.

- Do you push on through stress, tiredness and pain?

- Are you missing deadlines, forgetting to reply to emails?

- Are you competitive to the detriment of your health and relationships?

Do you allow others to find their way?

16

Surrender

How I learned the true meaning of surrender
in post-tsunami Thailand

One evening in March 2005 I was sitting in the camp manager's office in Khao Lak with some of the remaining foreign aid workers. He had called a meeting as he felt we had reached a new crisis point. We listened respectfully to this elderly Thai. He was clearly feeling under great pressure. He told us that the charity workers who had sprung to the aid of the Thai people after the tsunami were now leaving in droves.

'We began with 70,' he said. 'Now it's down to 20, and falling all the time. The hard fact is that the larger charities have already left.'

He didn't need to explain: we'd often spoken about it in the camps. The Thais, burdened by grief and despair, reliving the trauma of the wave, were quite unaware that a new crisis was looming.

'There's no work for these people. What are they going to do? They can't live on handouts forever.' Usually reserved and not one to show emotion, he put his head in his hands and his voice wobbled as he spoke. 'What is going to happen to these homeless people three months, six months, a year from now?'

I needed some quiet time to mull over his words. We had experienced the sheer momentum of the collective international response immediately following the crisis. Now we had to impress on businesses and individuals the importance of the recovery phase. They needed to be inspired to continue to contribute.

I for one wasn't giving up.

The devastation caused by the wave was only the beginning of the Thais' problems. For many of the people living on the southern coasts and islands, not only had their families, friends and homes been taken, but their livelihoods had also been washed away. Working in tourism had long been a predestined path for many. Schoolchildren knew their career options from a very young age: hotel gardener, cleaner, laundry worker, bellboy, assistant in a dive shop, perhaps a tour guide if they had a flair for English. The big wave had changed all that.

Ninety per cent of the local hotel workforce had been employed in the tourism industry. Now, 9000 hotel rooms had dropped to 900. More than half of the airport taxi drivers had lost their jobs, as had hundreds of bar staff, waitresses and diving instructors. With the sharp decline in tourist spending, thousands of jobs in the local communities were gone or at risk, and every week local merchants stood to lose millions of dollars. Most survivors did not have the money to repay their debts and resume their lives. Many had lost their homes and land and were forced to stay in relief centres. The few hotels that were rebuilding would not be ready for a couple of years.

I have always firmly believed that the only sustainable way out of poverty is through business. I had seen how handouts can vanish as quickly as if flushed down the toilet. It was a no-brainer; we simply had to support alternative business ideas for these workers. Tourism had always been a cash cow for the locals, but there had to be other sources of income they could turn to. What if we could encourage each vulnerable family to propose an income-generating project that suited their passion and skill set? We could then research it to determine if it was a viable plan and, if it was, help them get it off the ground. I knew I needed an ally. I called Miss Soonpon.

Miss Soonpon had been a teacher for over twenty years and was loved and respected by every family in the community. After the King and Buddhist monks, schoolteachers are the most trusted figures in Thai society. Miss Soonpon had taken on the role of social worker as well. Families with any type of social problem would wait patiently after school, knowing that from her they would receive practical and wise advice.

Her school was in a deprived area in the outskirts of Khao Lak, its 300 children drawn from poor families. The teachers had painted cartoons on the crumbling concrete walls, but this couldn't hide the general dilapidation of the place. Although many of the children's lives had been affected by the disaster, the building itself hadn't been damaged by the tsunami, so the school wasn't being supported by local charities. Determined to help the struggling families, Miss Soonpon was arriving early and staying after class to give them advice. She was unfailingly jolly, calm and practical, and I too came to rely on her heavily, barely making a move without consulting her first. Without her wisdom and inside knowledge, we probably would not have got the project off the ground.

Miss Soonpon was short and stocky. She wore large brown glasses that perched on the end of her nose to no obvious purpose as she always looked over them. Her short, spiky, grey-speckled hair gave her a jaunty look and she went everywhere with a broad smile, always with five or six children clinging to her skirt. They circled around her, holding her hand, skipping along beside her, gaining comfort from her presence. We met often. As she knew every family in the community, I was certain I could rely on her to come up with a list of those most in need. We decided that first she would announce our plan to everyone and then invite all those interested in getting involved to an interview at the school.

'They'll feel more comfortable there,' said Miss Soonpon. 'The staff room, after class has finished, will be perfect. They will be able to open their hearts.'

We were flooded with requests for help. By the end of the week Miss Soonpon's desk was heaped with papers in which people had poured out their hearts, sharing their crises. The stories were heartbreaking.

'Where do we start?' I asked. 'Every one of them needs help right now.'

Miss Soonpon said, 'Don't worry, Linda. I will take the letters home this weekend and select the first five families.' She beamed at me over her specs. 'They will all get their turn.'

To my surprise, when I arrived at the school early the following Wednesday afternoon all of the applicants were already waiting, sitting on the grass, talking and eating.

When I approached the group on the grass, I was offered a plastic bag of tea, which I accepted with thanks. I knew the street-seller. He had a stall outside the school gates. A painfully thin, elderly gentleman with a heavily lined, sunburnt face, he made the takeaway tea by first scooping crushed ice into a plastic bag, then pouring hot tea on top, which melted the ice. Last, with a few skilful twists and a flick of the wrist, he sealed the bag around a straw. Ingenious.

As I drank my tea I wondered how many simple yet clever ideas like this these families would be able to dream up with our help. The afternoon's interviewees filed in, family by family, fighting their shyness. Asking for help was their last resort: with every penny of their savings gone, they came because their backs were against the wall. They had nothing left.

The first family—parents and daughter—sat in a huddle on the sofa facing us, looking cowed. Miss Bani was dressed traditionally in a light batik sarong tied firmly in a knot around her waist. The colours in the fabric had faded to an indeterminate grey and held together by heavy darns. Her oversized white T-shirt was frayed at the neck. On the front and back was printed the slogan 'DTAC Happy', with the local phone company's logo, and beneath it a smiley face that jarred horribly with the wearer's anxious expression.

'Thank you for coming today,' Miss Soonpon said cheerily. 'You are among friends, so let us see how we can help you.' Her voice broke the tension in the room.

'We are so sorry to bother you, Teacher,' Miss Bani began, her eyes filling with tears.

'Never mind that,' replied Miss Soonpon, the schoolteacher in her taking control of the escalating emotion in a matter-of-fact way. 'Take a deep breath. Now tell us your story.'

The words came rushing out like a dam bursting its banks. 'I was a cook in a beachside hotel in Khao Lak. I love my job. I earn enough money to feed all of us. My husband had a car accident.' She pointed at his missing foot. 'This is our daughter, Puk. She's eight.' Puk was motionless, like a rag doll, eyes wide open, staring into space, head resting on her mother's lap. 'She hardly ever talks,' Bani stroked her daughter's head. 'She lost so many friends.'

Miss Soonpon nodded encouragingly.

'It was my day off. I was at the village pump doing the laundry. Thanks to Buddha we live at the foot of the mountain.' She glanced at her husband. 'We heard it coming. He can't run—but somehow we got him up the hill. The wave took all our possessions: our clothes, my daughter's school books, our food. Everything smashed, washed away, gone.

'The hotel is gone. There is nothing left.' Her shoulders slumped, but then she remembered what she had to say and sat upright, clearing her throat. 'Miss Soonpon, it's been six weeks now since I've worked and we can no longer feed our little girl.'

It was a difficult thing for a mother to say, and a difficult thing for us to hear.

'I cannot take care of her any more. There are no hotels for me to work in. It's all finished. Can you feed her?' (I wanted to scream, 'Yes!', to throw my arms around her and give her money for food. Sensing this, Miss Soonpon gestured for me to stay still.) Tears were streaming down her face now. 'I try to be strong, but I have to accept it that there is nothing I can do. I feel so ashamed.'

I took a breath. This wasn't the way. Giving money would be a bandaid solution at best. After two months the family would need money again.

Miss Soonpon took the lead. 'We understand your situation and we are going to help you, but not as you have asked.'

An agonised sigh came from the silent husband, as if a guillotine had just come down.

Khun Soonpon continued quickly, with a confident smile. 'Listen, it is *good* news. We are going to help you to set up a new business.'

At this, Bani looked even more upset. 'I am not a businesswoman! I'm a cook.'

On seeing the beads of sweat on his wife's face, her husband took her hand and squeezed it gently. I spoke then, hoping to reassure them. 'I know, but now is the time to look towards a different future, a new career.'

'I only know how to cook,' Bani repeated.

'Trust us. All we ask is for you and your husband to spend a few days thinking about your skills and your resources. How you would *like* to make a living if you could. Then look at your local community's needs and see whether your idea fits. This is how you will discover a new business idea. A way you can earn money and be independent again, and feed your family. You may not believe it possible right now, but surely it's worth a go. What do you think?'

Bani sat back and nodded. I could see she wasn't convinced but we had said enough for one day.

'Don't worry, we have a team of experts to help you think about what will work. They'll guide you. It's a new beginning.'

Miss Soonpon spoke quickly to the family in Thai. Her words were obviously reassuring, as their expressions relaxed a little. Then they rose and we all exchanged a customary *wai*, with heads bowed and palms together in front of our chests.

'See you in a few days,' I called after them as they walked away. The little girl turned and waved, with the tiniest hint of a smile.

Miss Soonpon called in the next family. I took a steadying breath. This was going to be one hell of an afternoon. I was relieved that we only had five families to see.

Miss Wati entered alone. She was a tiny woman, her fragile frame utterly swamped in her oversized clothes. A dirty gauze dressing, stained yellow with pus, was hanging loosely under her chin. Above it, her face was strained, with hollow cheeks and dark rings around her eyes. Miss Soonpon indicated gently where she should sit.

'I don't know where to start,' Wati mumbled quietly, head bowed. Her hands fiddled nervously with her bag. 'It's all such a mess.'

'We know. Just start when you're ready. Here, have a sip of water. We are here to help you,' the schoolteacher said.

'I worked in the laundry at a beachside hotel in Khao Lak. I have worked there for years. It's in the basement. I had come up for my normal break, to take some fresh air. It gets really hot down there with all the dryers. I was sitting on the grass deciding what to cook for supper when I heard a low rumbling noise, an odd sound I had never heard before.'

Wati's voice trembled and she paused for a sip of water. 'I saw a wall of water—it must have been 8 metres high—rushing straight towards me. It was like something from the movies. All I could hear was screaming, crashing, crunching.

'I remember thinking, I don't want to die. Not now. It's not my time! And I ran as fast as I could. But in my panic I ran back downstairs into the laundry. The wave followed me. I was like a doll in a washing machine. Round and round, over and over again. The pain in my ears and eyes was terrible. I heard my bones crack as they smashed against the walls. Something sharp ripped my skin. I could not breathe.'

Wati paused and lifted her arm, an action that took some effort, and touched the shaved concave area at the back of her skull.

'I was left lying in a pool of rubbish, coughing out the muck. The smell of sewage made me vomit. I knew I had to get out if I was to see my son again. One arm was useless. I don't know how I managed to get up the steps. Dragged myself on my stomach. Then luck smiled on me. A foreign man was running by and I threw myself in his way, grabbed his hand. The next thing I knew I was lying on the mountainside. I suppose the *farang* must have carried me there. I never saw him again but I thank Buddha every day for his kindness and pray for his soul.'

Wati fell silent and looked out of the window at her son playing football on the grass. Miss Soonpon leaned in close to me, speaking quietly. 'Wati has been in hospital since the tsunami. She was only released yesterday. She's had a lot of internal bleeding and she's still in a great deal of pain. She is also troubled with nightmares, depression and panic attacks. She tried to commit suicide, Linda. Her husband is still in hospital unconscious. They believe he was hit by a car.'

'Is that their only son?' I looked at the little boy playing outside.

'Yes, just the one child. He's five.' We explained to Wati about our plan for her.

She didn't flinch. 'Only one thing I know. I will never work close to that sea again.'

Leadership lesson #16

Surrendering in leadership can be viewed as weakness, but is it? Or is it a sign of confidence and belief? In surrendering, rather than hiding behind a role or a pre-determined plan, a leader can create a safe space for different outcomes to unfold. It takes courage and is not for the faint-hearted, because it involves radical letting go and trust. The aim is to influence, not control, to listen rather than tell. This allows team members to show their strengths and weaknesses, and empowers the reticent to shine.

***

Group intelligence can emerge from surrendering, drawing out inspiration and creativity, opening the natural flow of what 'wants' to happen.

- Do your team members feel comfortable sharing their ideas openly?

- Do you trust your staff enough to set them a goal while knowing they will find the right way to achieve it?

- Are you open enough to let things unfold even when you don't know what the outcome will be, what may emerge?

How can you see as others see
and feel as others feel?

17

Compassion

How I learned that success sometimes means being able to accept failure in post-tsunami Thailand

It was the beginning of a roller-coaster 18 months. At the start, I visited all our Thai families at least once every two weeks, and called them every week to check they had not hit any unseen obstacles in building their businesses. Very often they were bursting to share a new success with me. I had no idea at the beginning how long I would have to stay on this bruised and battered coastline, but one thing was clear: if anything was to be achieved, my physical presence was needed. My job was to broker the right partnerships, troubleshoot problems, give encouragement when obstacles got in the way and a sympathetic shoulder to cry on when it all became too much.

Above all, I was there to help provide the daily inspiration these new entrepreneurs needed to keep going forward and not give up. After all, these were a people not only embracing the challenge of starting anew but also bowed down by grief and haunted by their experience, many of them with debilitating physical injuries. In despair, some were driven to suicide, which was an entirely new phenomenon in their community and one that was confounding local leaders and the Thai government.

My daily fieldwork took me back to my days of district nursing when I had to try to juggle my patients, figuring out my timetable according to their geographic location and busy lives. In Thailand, I quickly got to know who got up early, ate late or had to pick up children from school. There were always unexpected events and emergencies I had to help with. Equipment would break; someone would have a last-minute hospital appointment; a mother would ask me to accompany her to the monastery to pray for her lost son. Then I would take out my red pen and rearrange my day. *Mai pen rai,* I would mutter to myself, trying to remain calm. *The best laid plans...*

As the number of families we were helping increased, my days became longer. Soon leisurely visits were out of the question. I found myself constantly checking my watch. My day always ended with a careful review of my notes. How were the families progressing? What was I missing? What else could we be doing? I would then email a concise report to my business team in Bangkok, who would study the figures and come back to me with any comments. I had to ensure that the team was kept abreast of any social, psychological and environmental factors that were affecting a family's livelihood recovery. As fieldworker, my job was to be the team's eyes and ears.

I appreciated the praise I received, but nothing came close to the joy Miss Soonpon and I felt when we visited individuals and families we had helped and found their lives had been changed for the better.

One time we ventured deep into the jungle to visit Lek, a five-year-old girl with HIV contracted from her mother, who had died of AIDS only a month before the tsunami killed her father. Now she was being cared for by her aunt Miss Piu. After the tsunami they had relocated deep in the jungle and were finding it impossible to make ends meet. Initially, Khun Soonpon had asked if we might be able to pay for Lek's HIV drugs to help the family. I hoped we could find a better solution.

Piu was a single mother, caring for her own two little girls as well as Lek, so she couldn't go out to work. When we first met it was clear that she was a bright and energetic young woman, open to starting her own business. It had taken her only a day to work out a viable plan. She told me the village where she lived was a considerable distance from the nearest garage and source of petrol. She thought she had spotted a gap in the market. My mind boggled: was she planning on erecting petrol pumps in her front garden?

As our truck made its way through the lush, jungle-covered mountains, ethereal mists swirled in the slowly warming morning air. I had taken extreme measures to ward off mosquitoes as I knew we'd be working in their playground. As well as wearing long trousers tucked into socks, boots and a long-sleeved, high-necked shirt, I engulfed myself in clouds of mosquito spray and an even more potent and toxic chemical repellent on my clothes and shoes.

When we reached the house I jumped out of the truck, already excited. I could sense that everything was going well. Lek came running up, giggling and clutching my leg. I picked up the little girl and gave her a big hug and we went into the house to look for her aunt.

Piu's idea had been to create a shed at the front of the garden in which she would place petrol drums and recycled coke bottles. Each would contain petrol, diesel or engine oil for motorbikes and farm vehicles.

The business brains in Bangkok had confirmed that it was a viable business that would allow her to earn money from home and at the same time care for her family. For less than $100 she purchased plastic drums, glass pumps and the wood to build the small outhouse. The news of Piu's new enterprise spread fast and her brother came from Surat Thani to see if he could help. Soon he was busy building the shed.

Piu was bursting to tell me how she was getting on. She held out her hands to greet me, standing tall.

'How is business?' I asked, although the question hardly needed asking.

'*Khop khun ka* [thank you], Linda, we did it! People love it. My customers are steady and regular. I even have enough to pay back the money I borrowed for Lek's drugs.'

We sat together on the step of her little house in the jungle and had tea. The atmosphere was magical. It was at moments like this I knew that everything we were doing was worthwhile.

Not every case was such a straightforward success story. Some of the people we were helping were much more fragile.

Miss Son had been working as a chambermaid at a beachside hotel on the morning the wave hit. Normally, the guests would have vacated their rooms, leaving them free for her to clean and tidy, but they'd been partying hard the night before. Miss Son was still finishing the first-floor rooms when she heard a deafening crash. She turned towards the noise. The last thing she recalls was seeing a poolside chair flying straight at her through the bedroom window.

Miss Son woke up days later in hospital. She had ingested so much dirty water her lungs had developed multiple abscesses. The doctors had feared this would kill her before she regained consciousness. They had pumped her full of IV antibiotics while friends kept a vigil at her bedside. When she came to, she was in agony. She had a dislocated left shoulder and a broken right arm, wrist and fingers. A pin was put in her arm and her wrist and fingers were put in plaster. But no matter what combination of painkillers the doctors put her on, they could not seem to control her pain.

We had to find a way to help her, as she was the breadwinner of the family. Her husband had died two years before in a bike accident and she was caring for her elderly parents and her five-year-old son. Thankfully, on the day of the tsunami the three of them had been away visiting relatives, far from the beach.

Miss Soonpon asked me to accompany her on a visit to Miss Son at home. 'Linda, this is a difficult situation. She is very sick but she is a proud lady. She wants to work.' She paused, looking worried. 'To be frank, I don't think it is possible, but if we don't try it I am afraid she will only get more depressed.'

Collecting some fruit on the way, Miss Soonpon and I took a local *tuk-tuk* to Miss Son's house. Her elderly parents were sitting outside on the wooden porch playing with Ralee, their little grandson.

'Have you come to see Mum?' Ralee said, grabbing Miss Soonpon's hand. 'She's in bed.'

We followed the boy into the house. We found his mother in a darkened bedroom.

'I am so happy you came. I am just getting up. I am fine.' Her voice sounded weak. 'I have a great business idea. Just need your help with it.' It was humbling to hear her words, so full of spirit. 'It's just the pain … if only I could control the pain I would be fine.'

We helped her get up. She winced every time she moved. 'Let's have some tea and I can tell you what I would like to do.'

We sat and listened carefully to her idea.

'I would like to set up a laundry business from my home. I have the space. It can be plumbed in here,' she said, pointing to a space in her outhouse. 'The garden is very sunny so the clothes will dry in no time. I love ironing.'

For a moment I was silent, unable to imagine her having the strength to lift an iron, let alone wet sheets and towels.

'The market is great,' she continued. 'Once I have the equipment—a washing machine, iron and ironing board—I will have customers. What do you think? Can you help me?'

Neither of us had the heart to demoralise this brave woman, but both of us were having the same thought.

Our silence alarmed Miss Son. 'I have no other choice. Please. I have no one else to help us.'

'I am concerned about your health,' Miss Soonpon said gently. 'What did the doctor say?'

'He said there is nothing more they can do. He hopes my body will adjust to cope with the pain. I'm sure he is right. I'll be fine … soon.'

Honestly, I doubted it. 'Is there any other, lighter business we can help you with?' I cast around wildly, hoping for inspiration.

'Linda, I don't feel strong enough to leave my house to sell things at the market or at school. If I work from home I know I have the option to lie down if the pain gets too much. My parents can always help.'

I very much doubted that too, given how elderly and frail they looked. 'Don't worry, we'll work something out,' I said with a confidence I didn't feel. 'Now, you go and get some rest.'

My business advisers were moved by Miss Son's plight but, like us, thought it likely her business would fail. The next week, against our better business judgement, we decided to give it a shot, while agreeing to build in extra support somehow. The equipment was bought and installed. When Miss Son saw her gleaming washing machine, iron and ironing board she smiled. For a fleeting moment her face looked softer, no longer tense from holding the pain.

'Start slowly—pace yourself,' I urged her. 'Just work a few days a week and see how you feel.'

Every other day I popped in to see how she was. At first, seeing the washing blowing on the line, I was encouraged. Maybe we were wrong and she'd be fine.

At the end of the second week, Miss Son called me in tears. 'I am so sorry. I cannot work this week. I know I am letting you down.'

'Of course you aren't,' I tried to reassure her. 'You've done brilliantly. Of course you'll have bad weeks. It's only to be expected.'

'You trusted me. And I am letting my family down, but the pain is too much. I give in. What is the point of living?'

I rushed straight to her home.

'You have been so brave,' I said, holding her gently in my arms. 'We tried too much too soon, that's all. Forget feeling guilty. We have to sort out this pain. I am going to Phuket International Hospital to get you an appointment and a second opinion. You are *not alone*, Miss Son.'

She put her head back on the pillow and slept.

The doctors and physiotherapists of Phuket International Hospital advised us that an intensive course of ultrasound treatment and daily physiotherapy might help. It was a gamble as her muscle damage was extensive. It took six months of therapy and daily visits to get Miss Son back on track. Her business remained small. She agreed to work only two days a week, to take on light laundry only, and to call one of her friends to help her if the pain became too great. She now earns enough to keep the family afloat, and a young niece is slowly taking over most of the workload.

These more difficult cases, men and women like Miss Son who had chronic physical or psychological problems, we formed into cooperatives. With a tight community support network they could call each other for help at times when they could not manage.

Three years after my first visit to Thailand I came back to see how the fledgling businesses were getting on. Virtually every one had taken off. Many had expanded; others had diversified. It was so heartening to see the entrepreneurial flame still burning strong.

When I visited Miss Bani, the first person we had interviewed in the schoolroom four and a half years before, I was greeted by a very different person from the despairing woman in the smiley-face T-shirt I had met with Miss Soonpon. She looked taller, calmer, more confident.

'Come, I want to show you something,' she said, taking my hand. She caught me looking at my flip-flops and understood my concern. Her house was on the edge of overgrown jungle and I was terrified of meeting a king cobra.

'You can borrow my husband's rubber boots. They should fit you.'

Bani led me silently down an avenue of tall trees. The forest was dense, the sun barely managing to break through the canopy. We finally reached a small clearing in which stood a sizeable wooden shed. As we walked up, her husband emerged from it and shook my hand.

'These rubber trees have been in our family for generations. We have 500. They produce at least eight sheets of rubber per day,' Bani told me.

'How much does that fetch?' I asked.

'A sheet sells for 50 baht. We earn about 400 baht a day.'

My business mentors had pointed out that rubber was an excellent way forward for those lucky enough to own land. It used to be a thriving local industry on the coast until tourism took over. The trees were there to be farmed and they were happy to invest in the pressing machines, tin trays and knives to make it happen. Thailand, they told me, is on track to become the world's biggest rubber exporter.

Beaming with pride, Bani told me that their weekly income was now four times greater than when they had worked in the tourism industry. And the business was growing all the time.

'My husband collects the sap each morning,' she told me proudly. 'Watch, he'll show you.'

Bani's husband took out a heavy curved metal knife that he had tucked in his leather belt. He held the point to the bark of the tree and, pressing hard, he carved a deep diagonal channel about a foot long around the trunk. Immediately a thick white gluey sap oozed out. Then, taking a half coconut shell which was hanging from a nail in the tree, he began to harvest the rubber.

'He has to work through the night with his team as the sap needs to be collected at the coolest time of day, before sunrise.'

I was then taken into the shed where we stood under rows of honey-coloured sheets the size of a bathmat. Bani showed me how the rubber is processed. She was like the captain of the ship now, in full sail. 'We then cut the rubber into sheets and put them through this old washing mangle to flatten and squeeze them even more. That's hard work.'

'How do you get them to market?' I asked.

'It's easy. An agent from a Bangkok rubber company comes to our door every two days.'

'You really have got things well sorted,' I said with admiration.

'Not just that,' she said proudly. 'We're now looking to get a machine to process glue. We're expanding the business all the time.'

As we walked back to the house I asked her how her daughter was getting along. I remembered the lifeless little girl burrowing into her mother's lap on the sofa at the school.

'She is so much happier. Her teacher says that she is much more lively at school, joining in with the others. Everyone says she is blossoming!'

When it was time for me to leave, Bani gave me a hug. 'We still talk every week to our business mentor, who gives us good advice,' she said. 'But we miss you, Linda.'

Another day I went to visit Miss Wati. For her, depression had been the most disabling aftereffect of the tsunami. Her body still bore the scars, but from the moment she had started her own business she came to life again. Wati liked to cook, and the more people appreciated her food, the more inspired she became.

'Your business people gave me 7000 baht to set up my mobile shop.'

'And how has it been going?' I asked her.

'It's very busy down at the construction sites. I've been worked off my feet. I can hardly produce enough to keep the men happy,' she said, smiling.

In the 18 months I had been working with the families I had kept up with her success. At first, she would call me every day, bursting with excitement, telling me that she had sold all her chicken in only a few hours.

'And have you managed to expand at all?' I asked.

'I've started to experiment with other foods. Cakes and salads. I cook the food I know they'll want to eat.'

'How is your son?'

'He's great. Got new shoes. And I've signed him up for the school trip,' she said proudly.

'I have been hearing such wonderful things about you,' I said, taking her hands in mine. 'You've been such an inspiration to everyone. You're a great business mentor, I hear. A real natural.'

'Who would have thought it?'

I knew she too was remembering the broken person we had met that day at the school, overcome by the hopelessness of her situation.

Leadership lesson #17

A compassionate leader helps others on their journey to self-awareness, courage, confidence and joy. A leader who shows the team they care will have no worries about loyalty or poor customer service. If a project goes awry, or an employee makes a disastrous mistake, it is easy to react with disappointment, anger or anxiety. Compassion is the fastest and most effective way to get back on a positive path that will move you and your company forward.

When your people feel safe in expressing their feelings and concerns, knowing you won't leap to judgement, you can figure out together how to navigate the most challenging situation. Compassion forges bonds and establishes trust. Prioritise taking care of your people over your bottom line. When you take care of your people, they will take care of your customers.

**

The key is to meet your people where they are, then offer yourself as a resource, not an opponent. Help them face and solve their problems. Roll up your sleeves and immerse yourself in the daily grind alongside your team. Let others see you serve, and encourage them to join you.

- Do you find it easy to see another's point of view?
- Do you prioritise the wellbeing of your people?
- What can you do this week to serve and care for your team?

Do you make judgements based on your own perspective or on multiple perspectives?

18

Through the eyes of another

How seeking and valuing another's perspective
saved the day in the Maasai Mara, Kenya

It was another glorious African day. The business leaders who had
signed up for my 'Be the Change' program had converged from the
four corners of the globe to see how they might make a difference
and empower the community. Excited that they would be visiting a
village and get to talk to the local Maasai today, they were eager to
get started.

The scenery was breathtaking, all around us an endless horizon with
the occasional single flat-topped acacia tree seemingly frozen in motion.

Led by Nelson, a local Maasai warrior, we left the jeeps behind and
walked towards the village in the distance marked by a semicircle of
low, thatch-roofed dwellings.

'Our homes are built by the women,' he said pointing at the small
village. 'Simple, traditional design. Made of mud and dung pasted over
a timber frame.'

'In my country,' commented Charles, from Texas, 'that would be
men's work.'

'Here women build the houses, carry the water, collect firewood and cook for their family,' Nelson explained. 'That's how it is.'

We entered the compound through a tall fence of thin saplings— designed to keep children, goats and cattle in and lions and other predators out, Nelson informed us.

Tall, lean men wrapped in bright red checked blankets started to appear from the loaf-shaped houses.

'Stunning colour,' said Emily, obviously dazzled by these impressive-looking warriors.

'Practical,' replied Nelson. 'Red scares away the lions.'

Soon our little group of six were surrounded by a circle of men and, at a distance behind them, an outer circle of women, who were quite as impressive as the men. Resplendent in bright, multicoloured cotton wraps, they had clean-shaven heads, high cheekbones, gleaming white teeth and beautiful black slanted eyes. Many had babies strapped to their backs and they swayed in unison. It was mesmerising.

The village scene was also captivating: the goats in the kraal, the shining pots and pans stacked high in the communal cooking area, the carefully laid out vegetable garden. David ducked into one of the mud huts through its tiny door, and exited fast, choking. 'Can't breathe in there—the wood smoke is trapped.'

'Where's the water pump?' Michael asked, looking around.

'There isn't one,' Nelson replied.

'So, we've found our first project!' A hugely successful entrepreneur, Michael was a man of action. He reached for his notepad and his phone. 'Where can we buy a pump? What will it cost? Who do we need to call to get this done right now?'

Under this barrage of questions, Nelson responded shortly, 'Let's finish our visit first,' and started to walk off towards the school. Meantime I had noticed the women's large, animated smiles had abruptly turned to frowns.

What's this about? I asked myself. *What did Michael say to trigger such a change in mood?*

I let the group trail off in single file behind Nelson, while I approached the women, who now stood in a discontented huddle.

'What's the matter?' I asked.

They turned to greet me, but no one spoke.

'Please tell me, don't be shy. I want to know.'

They looked at each other uneasily. One woman dared to catch my gaze and spoke up. 'We don't want a pump in the middle of the village.'

'Why ever not?' I asked.

After a brief silence, she replied, 'A woman's life is hard here. Many chores.' The other women nodded in agreement. 'We are trapped in this compound, Linda. We cook, clean, take care of the homes and children.' She paused and looked around the small enclosure. 'We love walking to collect the water. It gives us the freedom to leave this space. Sometimes we take a picnic to share with our sisters. Sometimes we even meet our boyfriends!' The light came back into this group of warrior women and they giggled like naughty schoolgirls. 'If you install a pump in the village, all of this is taken away from us. Please don't do this.'

I reflected on the danger of my first-world assumption. We imagined we knew the best solution, because it's what we would have wanted.

Leadership lesson #18

Our perspective or point of view is shaped by our cultural values, life experiences, assumptions, current state of mind and many other influences. Sometimes we share it with others, sometimes not. A perspective is not right or wrong by default, but it does shape how we act or react in any situation.

We readily see our perspective as aligning with reality, 'the way things are'. But reality tends to be a subjective construct. Seeking out different perspectives is an essential leadership skill. Imagine the point of view of one of your staff. Ask yourself, *As an employee, what do I want? What do I fear?* Then adopt a different perspective —say, that of a manager or executive. How would your answers change? This skill allows you to understand past situations and make better decisions now for the future.

***

Considering different viewpoints contributes to our understanding of a situation and helps our decision making. Being authentically curious about others' perspectives can often reveal potential blind spots or new solutions.

- As a leader, do you tend to consider your own perspective as representing 'objective reality'?

- How much weight do you give to the impact of a decision or situation on those you lead?

- Have you explored their perspective so you can respond creatively based on your new understanding?

Part IV

Awareness

The ultimate value of life depends upon awareness and the power of contemplation rather than upon mere survival.

Aristotle

Are you ready for your next challenge?

19

Be prepared

How lack of preparation nearly killed me
in Tibet

How could I help with the health problems in Tibet that His Holiness
was so concerned about? After our meeting at Mindrolling Monastery
in late 2002, I turned the challenge around in my head as I bounced
along in the crowded bus back to Delhi.

Tibet was a notoriously harsh environment, especially in the High
Himalayas where the worst of the problems were found. Many of the
remote areas in greatest need were almost inaccessible, far from towns
or villages with even the most basic resources. Food supplies, medical
backup and communications were limited to nonexistent.

I knew what I wanted: medically skilled and adventurous young
people who would be sensitive to the Tibetan culture and the
complexities of the Chinese occupation. By the end of my bus trip I
had it. Second-year medical students from training hospitals who were
looking for overseas placements for their final year would be perfect.
There would have to be a careful selection process. I'd need to find
individuals who were tough, resilient and resourceful.

I was keyed up with excitement and could hardly wait to start
organising things. When a cow ambled into the road and the bus
swerved violently to avoid it, I was jolted back into the present.
Catching the eye of the lady sitting next to me, dressed in a colourful

sari and lovingly nursing a chicken in her lap, I smiled. Over the next few weeks it became clear to me that thorough planning would be needed before I could let students loose in the Himalayas. My only knowledge of the area had been gleaned from the accounts of some of the first great Western explorers of Tibet—intrepid, inspirational figures like Alexandra David-Néel. They had coped so admirably with the challenge of that harsh, inaccessible terrain without the most basic comforts. But could I?

The more I researched the medical problems Tibetan women faced, the stronger grew my determination to help them. Tibet has one of highest newborn and infant mortality rates in the world. Women there are 300 times more likely to die than Westerners from complications due to pregnancy or delivery. Postpartum haemorrhage is the leading cause of death. Similarly, babies are far more likely to die in Tibet than anywhere else in the world. But what really fired my determination to help was the fact that most of these deaths are preventable with minimal technology and simple interventions.

The vast majority of births take place at high altitude in a cold environment and without access to electricity or healthcare. More than 90 per cent of women give birth at home. Of those, 54 per cent are attended by female relatives, while only 13 per cent rely on healthcare providers. Curiously, Tibetan society is one of the few in the world in which there is no tradition of trained midwives to facilitate the delivery process. Poor nutrition and the lack of trained health personnel and emergency services combine to place Tibetan women and infants at high risk for labour-related deaths.

A Tibetan mother's death is devastating to her family: it often threatens the health of her children and can impact the family for generations. The mother is considered the thread that holds the family together. When she dies prematurely, her surviving children are three to ten times more likely to die within two years. And they are less likely to attend school or complete their education. Many Tibetans believe that a mother's death during childbirth is ominous: a sign of bad spirits gathering to wreak misfortune on her family and community.

In Tibetan nomadic communities, most babies are delivered with only the help of the pregnant woman's mother or mother-in-law, and then the only assistance they give is in the cutting of the cord. I was horrified to learn that many Tibetan women deliver their babies completely alone. The cold statistics pointed to an urgent need for action.

My eagerness to jump straight in and get on with it, combined with my innate belief that 'everything will be all right', meant my first trip to the High Himalayas nearly ended in disaster. It had taken me two days in a jeep, mostly 'off-roading' on dirt tracks, to reach my mountain guides. I was inappropriately dressed, had never ridden a horse before, and was sorely lacking in sensible provisions and medical equipment.

We set out from Chengdu with the rain beating down on us. Our jeep bounced along the snaking road, driving precariously around piles of mud and stones from rockslides, past overturned trucks, abandoned tractors and vehicles bogged in mud, halting often when sheep and wild yak crossed our path.

As we started to climb into the mountains the scenery changed dramatically. We passed blood-red cliffs and wove around vast barley fields. In the villages, outside the two-storey whitewashed mud-brick houses, colourful prayer flags snapped in the stiff breeze. We entered a vast, empty and forbidding landscape that looked as if it was caught in a medieval time warp, where mysterious fortified castles jutted bleakly from the rock. Who knows why they were built this way, whether as a defence against human enemies or wolves, or simply as a barricade against the howling, freezing winds?

The Tibetan caravan was waiting for me at the agreed rendezvous point. This was the company that would lead me to the nomads I would be working with who were camped in the high mountains. My guides were enjoying the afternoon sun, their yaks and mules grazing around them. They were chatting contentedly, drinking tea and eating *tsampa*, a delicious staple food of the region made of roasted barley flour and salted butter tea mixed by hand.

My assembled guides were a mix of tall, dark-skinned women with sturdy limbs and wind-scoured faces, wearing deep-hued homespun robes under rainbow-striped aprons, and tall, stocky men in dirt-stiffened *chubas*, their braided hair rolled into a bun. I knew there was nothing extravagant about the harsh lives of these gentle souls who lived in such an inhospitable land, yet as if in mockery of this thought, I was dazzled, as always, by the sheer brilliance of their coral, turquoise and silver jewellery.

My arrival caused a buzz of excitement as the horsemen and -women made final preparations for the journey. Scruffy-maned, unshod mules and yaks stood placidly while more and more gear was thrown onto their backs. First, a crude wooden frame lashed together with rope was perched on the animal's back and tied firmly under its belly. Onto this odd-looking saddle were draped large hessian sacks of provisions such as tea and wheat, then blankets, rugs and a sleeping pad.

How on earth am I ever going to straddle all that? I thought to myself. *Great padding for my posterior—no chance of saddle sores—but I may just dislocate my hip!*

'Jump up,' directed my guide.

We edged the mule close to a large boulder, which I used as a mounting block before being pushed and pulled until somehow I reached my lofty perch, my legs dangling over the many layers of supplies, the mule somewhere far beneath. We set off in bright sunshine, ambling alongside of a gentle, babbling brook. I soon felt totally at ease. My mule was sixth in the long caravan train and I felt perfectly safe and secure. With the sun warm on my back, and lulled by the hypnotic sound of the Tibetans' chanting, I nearly fell asleep.

Abruptly, I sensed a change of direction and I looked around to reorient myself. The gentle stream on my right had become a Himalayan torrent, fast-flowing and fierce. I pushed myself up on my stirrups so I could see over the shoulder of the rider in front of me. In horror, I watched as the lead mule plunged straight into the river. My mind was in turmoil: 'No, I can't do that!' I looked up and down the river in desperation. There was no bridge in sight. I needed to get someone's attention. I twisted round but met only the nonchalant gaze of the heavily laden yak behind. I bellowed in an effort to get the attention of the rider in front of me. Nothing. The noise of the river smothered everything but the pounding of my heart. My turn had come. We slid sideways into the icy-cold mountain water with a frightening splash. I shut my eyes and held on so tightly that every muscle in my body tensed. My mule lurched downwards and struggled to find his footing. My boots filled with icy river water.

I started to repeat the Tibetan mantra that I had heard so many times: *Om mani padme hum*—'Praise to the jewel in the lotus'. I prayed as never before.

The current was so strong it was seizing my legs, dragging me from my saddle. Someone was shouting but, with the roar of the river and the seething panic in my head, I couldn't make it out. I held on with all my strength, my mind focused intently on just two things: protecting my camera and passport, and staying on the mule.

Then it was over. I was thrown sharply backwards as my trusty mount scrambled up the bank, gurgling and spitting water. I had survived. The shouting changed to clapping and I opened my eyes. Dry land. I felt as high as a kite, sailing on the crest of an adrenalin rush. Indiana Jones...on a clop-foot nag.

Now we were climbing so steeply we had to dismount. When I lost my footing on the loose gravel a firm, rough hand grabbed mine, pulling me along. Still feeling relieved after the river crossing and comforted by my companion's strength, I had no idea how much worse things would get.

As we reached the rise, the blue skies began to turn black. We pressed on as if trying to outpace the storm. Then it hit us: the wind whipped up furiously and the rain battered down in unforgiving, ice-cold sheets. With visibility down to zero, the caravan did not stop. There was nowhere to hide from this. We had to keep moving forwards.

By now I was slumped on the back of my mule, wailing. My head was pounding from altitude sickness and I was soaked through, my yak-hair blanket doing nothing to stem the flow of the icy water running down my back. I was shivering uncontrollably, pleading, though no one could hear: 'Please let me get off. Please just let this be over.'

I remember that the horsemen tied me down and put a heavy blanket over me, but after that I must have lost consciousness.

'What's happening to me? Where am I?' My numbed brain was confused.

I could feel my naked body being rubbed vigorously by several pairs of rough hands. I breathed in the pungent smell of rancid butter and heaved. My body was so stiff and bruised that it felt like I was lying on a bed of stones—I could feel a thousand sharp edges digging into me. I tried to sit up but hadn't the strength to lift my head. In the feeble glow of butter lamps I saw the faces of women peering down at me.

From their clothes I realised they were nuns. One had lit a fire in what looked like a small saucepan, and was wafting it continuously up and down over the length of my body. They did not speak to me and never once stopped the rhythmic rubbing of my body. As they worked they chanted softly. I slipped in and out of consciousness, but at no point was I afraid. I felt, instead, a profound sense of peace and a relaxed acceptance of fate. I drifted off to sleep to the sound of thunder and the rattle of hailstones against the tent.

As dawn broke, I woke to the sound of giggling. Young children were peeping curiously into the tent. It was apparent they had seen few white faces in their lifetime and this was too good an opportunity to miss. I found out that our caravan had stumbled across a small company of *Drokpas*, nomadic shepherds living in black yak-hair tents, who had taken us in and the nuns who were living with them helped saved my life. To my complete surprise I felt completely recovered that morning. Their medicine had been extraordinarily effective.

'Can you ride?' my guide asked me in sign language. I nodded.

Ignoring the Tibetan custom of making only the most conservative of farewells, I gave each nun an enormous Western hug before clumsily mounting my mule. Words could never have expressed what I felt. As our caravan of yaks and mules set off, I looked back for a final time at the small group gathered by the tents. I knew I had experienced the most precious of things: love and healing bestowed by people who gave freely, without expecting anything in return.

The experience had made me more committed than ever to bring the medical students here to work with these compassionate people who were surviving against such heavy odds. We would do our bit to help the Tibetans, one birth at a time. I started to formulate a better plan, one that would ensure my team were well prepared with the right resources and adequate backup. I was already making lists in my head:

- layered clothing works best—thermals, polar fleece vests, cotton T-shirts
- yak-hair poncho (to be ordered from Tibetans in advance—one per person)
- head torch (need hands free!)
- high-energy snack foods
- toilet paper
- warm sleeping bag
- waterproof bags for passport/camera/dry socks
- sunscreen (waterproof and highest protection factor available)
- industrial-strength lip gloss (to avoid sore lips from the sun and wind)
- silk long johns and underwear (against chafing)
- talcum powder (also to help with chafing)
- a waterproof hat (one you can tie on in the wind)

- sunglasses

- wet wipes (washing is usually not an option)

- perfume or essential oils such as lavender (for calming and disguising a multitude of unwelcome smells—see previous point!)

- a towel that packs down and dries quickly (highly recommended)

- a sense of humour (most important of all).

Leadership lesson #19

When entering an unfamiliar space, observe what the locals do. Learning about the environment, the people and the difficulties you may face will help you to adapt quickly and make wiser choices. This reduces the risk of making mistakes that impact people negatively. It also ensures that the people feel safe under your leadership. Moving into an unfamiliar environment, emotional preparation is as important as local knowledge. Leadership is not all about you.

Always think and move forward. As a leader, you must be prepared for the unexpected. Don't let failure defeat you; rather, allow it to guide you back onto the right track.

**

Preparing well means being a great listener, being resilient and mentally prepared, and being ready for the future while staying on point in the present.

- How quickly could you come up with Plan B if your current plan fails?

- If a key person in your organisation leaves, are you prepared or will it leave you vulnerable?

- What if your key customer/client leaves? Do you have enough business with others to weather the loss, or might you find yourself out of business?

How often do you put your
people before yourself?

20
Empathy

How slipping on their shoes (or *burkha*) allowed me to connect and be seen

I had the most unlikely of allies during my time in Pakistan, one who was to become my staunchest friend. My driver, Faisal, was a Pashtun from Swat Valley, near the Afghan border. Taliban country. Faisal belonged to a community where women would be chastised for showing their face in public, let alone travelling unaccompanied and bossing farmers about. Initially, Faisal had a strictly professional concern for me as his passenger (and meal ticket), but over the months this grew into real mutual affection and respect. He often offered me advice and increasingly engaged in the work I was doing. A wiry man in his late twenties with a thick black beard and moustache, he had a wife and three small boys back home, a hundred miles from Islamabad, whom he got to visit only every few months.

I learned many rules to protect my safety, but I disregarded the one that stipulated you should change your driver frequently. Keeping the same driver was a known hazard. Any employee who knew too much about your daily habits and schedule could be used by terrorists. Keeping Faisal, though, was a risk I was prepared to take. From the first, I liked his air of calm and attention to detail. The moment I exited a building he was by the car door, ready for me to slip away. His initiative saved me on numerous occasions. And he was the one who dried my tears when things became too much. Faisal was the one person in Pakistan who kept me smiling.

It was to Faisal I went for help when I needed to buy a *burkha*. I was getting ready for my first trip to the dairy country of northern Sindh province. I would be going alone. My assignment was to assess the most practical ways we might help organise scattered dairy farmers into cooperatives. If I was to have any chance of persuading them to listen to me, I needed to do my best to fit in with local custom, and that meant wearing a *burkha*. So I asked for Faisal's help.

In the shop, we scanned the rails. 'What about this?' I held up a pale blue cotton *burkha*.

He gave it a quick glance. 'No, madam. That is an Afghan *chadri*.' He told me that Westerners call it a shuttlecock *burkha*. 'You'll need that when you go to the North-West Frontier Province. Or in Peshawar or the refugee camps. Not Sindh.'

I could see why it was called a shuttlecock *burkha*. The top was shaped to grip the head and looked just like the top of a shuttlecock. There was just a small area covered by woven latticework for the eyes.

'How on earth do you get around? My eyesight's bad enough as it is.'

'It's an art, madam,' he said, before adding as an afterthought: 'My grandmother was knocked down by a car. She didn't see it coming.'

I smiled to myself as I watched Faisal handling the *burkhas*. He was becoming increasingly absorbed in his task. As fastidious as a Savile Row tailor.

'Look at the trim,' he held out one with a small diamante YSL logo. 'Hmm, perhaps not suitable for Sindh farmers.' He handed me one with a mandarin collar. 'I think this will be long enough. We can't have your walking boots showing.'

I gave a twirl as I exited the changing room. 'What do you think?'

I had thought the *burkha* looked like a shapeless dressing gown, but Faisal's eyes lit up with delight.

'Oh, madam! You look beautiful!'

Faisal had seen me in a variety of practical outfits — trousers and shirt or tunic — all, to my mind, perfectly attractive. But the *burkha!* It blew him away. You could see it in his eyes.

'Now try on the *hijab*. You must cover your blond hairs.' I could never persuade Faisal to use 'hair' rather than 'hairs' — he would always argue his case logically and vehemently.

A few minutes later my hair, ears, neck and chest were covered with the *hijab*. Faisal stood back to admire his work.

'Beautiful, madam!'

Leadership lesson #20

True leadership demands a willingness to place others' needs above your own. Empathy means understanding another's perspective, experience and feelings. It opens doors and minds, removing confusion and softening hearts. Openness foils defensiveness. The compassionate, empathic leader can solve problems creatively in ways that drive productivity and long-term success.

To ensure we are truly seen and heard may require us to change—whether it's our body language, our approach or, sometimes, even our appearance!

***

Before criticising someone, try to imagine yourself in their shoes. Set your sights on caring more than you thought possible. Sound hard? It simply means being genuinely curious and interested.

- Are you able to see things from another's point of view?

- Do you really care about your team? What do you know about their home situation, their hopes and dreams?

- Do you take the time to ask questions and listen?

Women leaders, Pakistan

Do you find yourself complaining, 'I can't, I don't have the resources'?

21

Learn and improvise

How I was forced to be flexible in the foothills of Himalayan Tibet

Following my first trip to the Tibetan nomadic communities, and drawing on my nursing background, I decided to form a small medical taskforce to run a childbirth awareness program in the Himalayas. I invited second-year medical students from Bristol University Medical College in the UK to accompany me. My candidate interviewing technique was unorthodox. Instead of firing up the students with descriptions of all the wonderful things they would see and experience, I painted an exceedingly daunting picture. My intention was to attract individuals with the right level of courage and determination and to weed out those who would be so overwhelmed by the demands made on them that they would want to come straight home. I knew it would need a special type of person to slip quietly and effortlessly into the harsh reality of life in the Himalayas, with its hardships and political and cultural sensitivities.

I placed the ads and waited. Within a few days I received five applications and arranged to meet the students in a local café in Bristol.

Alice was the first to arrive. A tiny, elegant girl with waist-length hair and wide eyes, she beamed at me and sat down, almost disappearing behind her enormous leather satchel. Words tumbled out: 'I am so excited to work with you. I was born in Hong Kong, I speak fluent Mandarin and am a human rights activist.' She barely drew breath and although I admired her enthusiasm, something worried me. Then Steve arrived. 'Am I late?' he asked anxiously. From the sweat on his forehead I realised he must have run all the way from the university. He collapsed into the nearest chair, easing out his long legs into the available space. 'My friend will be here any minute—we've been playing rugby and he's hurt his head.' Finally John, an athletic-looking redhead, arrived.

I glanced at my watch, it didn't look like anyone else was going to show. I looked at the three eager young faces in front of me and tried to envisage how they would fit in. They looked so at home in the café with their coffee and cookies. What would they make of the High Himalayas, where the only available snack food would be dried yak cheese washed down with yak butter tea? No comfy chairs, no heating and certainly no Western plumbing. 'Have any of you travelled to the Himalayas?' I asked. 'India, Nepal, Pakistan?'

'I climbed Mount Kenya last year,' Steve offered. 'It was great!'

'Well, I'm going to give you as much background as I can today, so you can make an informed decision. Our mission is to teach safe childbirth practices to villagers who have no access to medicines or midwives and who use a dirty knife to cut the umbilical cord. You will find their beliefs and the way they do things strange. You'll be immersed in an alien culture and you'll need to work with them sensitively. They don't speak English so unless you learn Tibetan, you'll be relying on miming for communication, so you'll need to be as good at acting as you are at medicine.' Nervous laughter followed.

I continued to test their reactions. 'How would you feel about having no communication with the outside world for a month—no phone, no internet, no electricity, no access to news or media?'

John looked shocked. 'You mean we can't call home at all?' he asked with an involuntary glance at his mobile phone.

Alice leaned forward quickly, almost knocking over her coffee. 'But how do we charge our computers and camera batteries if there's no electricity? How do we document it all for our coursework?'

It was going to take a while for it all to sink in.

'It's back to basics. Notepad and pencil are best.' I ploughed on. 'If you do decide to come you'll have no running water, very basic food—no fruit or vegetables, no salads. You'll be sleeping in basic shelters, often tents, sometimes with the goats and yaks.' Their eyes widened but they didn't interrupt. 'You'll be living and working at altitudes over 5000 metres. Think of everything you take for granted in your lives—and toss it away.'

After a few moments to let all that sink in, I changed course and told them what a huge difference their presence would make.

Alice was the first to speak. 'I've heard the nomads' pain threshold is extraordinary. It's going to be exciting!' I smiled at her, impressed by how swiftly she'd moved from trepidation back to enthusiasm. I looked at the others and waited for their reaction. John was next. 'Nothing I've heard has changed my mind,' he said with a grin. 'I'll just have to fill my rucksack with chocolate.' Steve agreed.

'Unless you have any questions, let's call it a day. I'll email you the necessary forms and a packing list. You'll see that "humour and flexibility" is at the top—for very good reason!'

Six months later, in August 2003, I returned to the Himalayas accompanied by Steve and John. They arrived at the airport laden with comfort food and thick novels, which they jokingly said would double as pillows. They were already growing beards. 'What's the point in shaving?' Steve declared with a shrug. I suddenly felt light-hearted. Yes, it would be a responsibility guiding these two young students, but it would be fun too, and with that we boarded the plane to Chengdu.

Guided by the brilliant work of One Heart, an American NGO, our remit was to introduce to the nomadic mountain communities practical skills for keeping mothers and babies safe. In the absence of trained birth attendants we would have to enlist and inspire whoever was available—aunts, nuns, even granddads. I knew that with the right approach we could save lives.

The journey to the first remote communities took two days by jeep and several hours on foot. Finally, we arrived at the first rendezvous point and set up camp on a hillside next to a flowing aqueduct of clear water...and waited. Steve and John took out a pack of cards and were soon rolling around on the grass fighting and laughing, blissfully unaware of my anxiety. Would anyone from the community come?

I scanned the horizon for signs of movement, but the high plateau was still, except for a few large birds circling overhead. No formal communication system operated here—no phone, internet, radio or television—so perhaps no one had received the message that we were coming. I approached our translator and local guide, Tsering. 'Be patient,' he smiled. 'Everything will happen as it should.'

I lay back on the cool grass and closed my eyes, trying to quell my misgivings. Suddenly the ground began to shudder as if the gods were drumming the earth. I leapt to my feet to witness the sight of a monk galloping towards us at breakneck speed, his saffron robes flowing out dramatically behind him. What a glorious sight! He pulled up with a flourish and leapt down, dragging a large saddlebag behind him. One by one he drew items out of his bag. On a thick rug he placed a bright yellow piece of silk, carefully smoothing it flat with his hands, a conch shell, an ornately carved bell, and a book of scriptures. Then, seated in the lotus position, his head lowered and eyes closed, he started to rock back and forth, chanting quietly.

The three of us watched, entranced. Meanwhile, a young boy who had accompanied the monk brought twigs and leaves and lit a small fire, reaching into the saddlebag for juniper and incense to throw into the flames. He looked up, glanced in our direction and smiled.

An hour passed. We gazed at the incense spiralling upwards, twisting and turning. Then, as if drawn by the magic of the ceremony, the silence was broken and a crowd started to gather. Appearing first as silhouettes on the mountain ridge, dressed in colourful, traditional clothes, they came on horses and mules, on motorbikes with red and yellow ribbons streaming from the handlebars, by truck and on foot. It felt like a dream.

A woman appeared on horseback with her young infant strapped to her back; a man sat astride a huge black yak with his young daughter in tandem. Another nomad twirled a prayer wheel. Then came a procession of old and disabled men and women, many carried on the backs of strong young men. And all around, darting back and forth, weaving in and out of the line of people, countless giggling rosy-cheeked children.

A pot was suspended over a fire and was soon bubbling with tea. Bottles of *chang*, a locally brewed alcoholic drink, were piled up in one corner. Everyone contributed something. Small circles of men formed on the grass, some chatting, some weaving. Steve turned to me. 'What do we do now?' We were sitting apart from the nomads and sensed that we had reached a point where we needed to begin or we might lose our audience. I was not going to let that happen.

'Don't worry,' I said, 'I've a few tricks up my sleeve.' Little did they know that I meant this quite literally.

I rummaged through my pack for my little magic bag, always a great ally in times like this, whether as icebreaker or crowd-puller or, when needed, a tool to resolve conflict and calm tense situations. I pulled out several large, colourful silk scarves—red, gold and blue—and waved them in big circles above my head. This immediately caught the attention of the children, who stopped and stared in surprise. I laid the scarves on the ground and took out three wide-mouthed cups—one yellow, one red and one blue—and three small red balls. I beckoned to the children to come closer, but they did not move.

With several theatrical taps of my magic wand I started the performance. The balls passed through the solid bottoms of the cups, jumping from cup to cup only to reappear in another or to vanish completely. Out of the corner of my eye I saw Steve and John looking a little embarrassed, as if witnessing a mad aunt behaving badly, but the people were mesmerised. Not just the children, but also the women who peeped out shyly from behind the men, and the elders with their toothless grins.

I laid it on for more than twenty minutes. Afterwards, Steve strode up to me and put his arm around my shoulders. 'You're a dark horse, Linda,' he said. 'We'll have to watch you. Who knows what else you're going to pull out of that bag of yours?'

'Well, the ice is broken. Let's get the job done, shall we?' And with that I picked up two of my teaching aids — a plastic baby doll and a picture-based flipchart.

The translator announced the start of the program and the crowd listened intently. 'Shouldn't we encourage the women to come forward?' John whispered. 'Surely they are our target audience … not these old men.' I looked at the motley assortment of granddads, uncles and brothers gathered at the front and at the women hiding some way off behind the menfolk.

'Tsering, please ask the group to form a circle and sit down on the grass.' Steve and John circled around like sheepdogs guiding their flock while I spread out a large towel and Sally, our plastic demonstration doll, inside the circle. Steve and John knew their cue — it was their time to take centre stage. John, by far the more outgoing of the two, became ringmaster, doing a quick spin around the group, breaking into a skip. '*Tashi delek* — hello,' he shouted. Meanwhile, Steve deftly set up the flipchart and prepared the props. The circle started to get smaller, closing in on them with curiosity. Within just a few minutes Steve and John were in the swing of things and I could relax and enjoy the show.

For hours the students patiently acted out their lessons in different groups, using diagrams on the flipchart and dynamic roleplay. It was exciting to see how keen the locals were to learn; they asked so many questions and took turns in the middle of the circle, holding the baby doll, practising clearing out its mouth and nose, and carefully placing it inside their tunics. The afternoon was punctuated by frequent bursts of laughter.

That day and for the next few weeks we taught basic hygiene to different community groups, including hand washing, bathing the baby, even breast-feeding techniques. The people were hungry to learn; they never got bored, even when we kept coming back to the three key messages. Soon they were chanting them like a mantra: '*Use a clean knife! Clear the airways! Keep the baby warm!*'

At one point I noticed that a pretty, young girl had become totally besotted with Steve. She would not leave his side and gazed at him devotedly, touching his hair while he was trying to demonstrate baby-care techniques. He was getting more and more flustered and clearly had no idea how he should handle it. Red in the face, he turned to his friend. 'Right! Over to you, mate. I'm off to teach tooth-brushing,' and in a flash he had scarpered to the children's group, deftly avoiding the clutches of his admirer. 'Steve's got a girlfriend!' I heard John sing out to his hastily departing back. By now the two students had been elevated to guru status.

Our translator had made it clear to the community that we were there solely to teach mother and baby care. But the presence of skilled medical practitioners made it inevitable that every type of ailment would be presented, from rickets to blindness. Although I had predicted this, it was still overwhelming. We saw people with club feet, TB, skin infections and badly broken limbs. 'This is crazy!' Steve was close to panicking. 'Most of these cases we've only read about in a textbook. I'm really not sure I can do this.'

John put his hand on Steve's shoulder. 'Yes you can. Look, we are probably the best they've ever had. We'll take it slowly, see them together, pool our knowledge.' It was amazing to watch the resourcefulness of this pair. One by one they examined each person, offering what advice they could, slowly working their way through the line of patients. Then it was done. The day was over. 'I need an ice-cold beer,' John declared as he slumped down on the grass, exhausted. They both looked utterly drained, emotionally and physically. I congratulated them both on what they had achieved, but Steve still looked upset.

'We were rubbish. We had no way of doing it properly, no way of checking the signs and symptoms. If only we could have done more!'

I couldn't bear to see Steve disheartened. 'Just look at them, Steve.' Even though it had been a long day, the locals were still with us and in small groups were excitedly discussing what they had learned. 'They'll put what we've taught them into practice. It's what we came for.' The crowd lingered, reluctant to leave, but the sun was setting and the wind was picking up. Most had a very long journey home.

We spent two months in the region, teaching first aid and basic hygiene, and of course patients with all kinds of conditions continued to arrive in a steady stream. John and Steve thrived on the experience, but it was tough at times. The food and sleeping arrangements were challenging, the whole experience an extreme culture shock for them. But these challenges soon faded into the background as we were joyfully embraced by the communities and even invited into their homes as honoured guests.

The trip was a success because John and Steve had the courage to step out of their comfort zone into an alien environment far removed from their day-to-day lives. They embraced the nomadic way of life, improvised where necessary, got the job done as best they could with what they had and worked as a team, pooling their medical knowledge, and supporting and encouraging each other.

After two months John and Steve finally headed home, infinitely richer for their incredible Himalayan experience.

The simple techniques we shared with the communities continue to be practised and are being handed down to the next generation. This is John and Steve's legacy to these amazing communities.

Leadership lesson #21

As a leader, you will often find yourself in situations you didn't choose, bound by the decisions and actions of others, without the resources or relevant training you need. You have many options moving forward, but no clear rules to tell you what the right one is. The secret to success lies in a positive and flexible mindset, involving the team and their expertise, improvisation and innovation.

In our fast-paced world, we don't always have the opportunity to learn before executing a plan; sometimes we must learn *while* executing. Lack of knowledge can itself be an important source of learning. Stop feeling the need to be perfect before taking action. Lack of fear fuels experimentation. Too much structure kills innovation.

***

Prepare yourself to take full ownership of a challenging situation even when the possibility of failure looms. Open yourself up to learning from others and embracing an environment in which your team improvises a solution.

- How adaptable are you?

- How do you feel if you need to undertake a task without the relevant knowledge and resources?

- Do you believe that accepting imperfection could take your team to a higher level?

Do you trust your gut feeling?

22

Intuition

How elephants became my greatest teachers in post-tsunami Thailand

We had reached the beach now and everywhere we saw the ugly toll the tsunami had taken. I looked along the debris-strewn strand and paused, placing a hand on my new friend Judd's arm.

'Look—over there. Elephants!'

As we drew closer, we saw that some were clearing rubble or transporting heavy cutting equipment while others were carrying sheet-wrapped corpses tied to their tusks. It brought tears to my eyes to see these gentle giants going about their work with such grace and care.

'Did you know that not one animal bone was found post-tsunami,' Judd said. 'No dog or cat bones. They knew the wave was coming hours before it arrived. The elephants' owners were astonished when for no apparent reason, three hours before the wave hit, they pulled up their stakes and slowly started to walk up the mountainside.'

I had always heard that animals have a sixth sense, some sort of vibrational awareness, that humans have long since lost.

Trusting a gut feeling didn't come easy to me at the start of my aid career. I've no doubt that frequently finding myself in volatile situations fast-tracked the honing of my faith. Experience taught me that conscious reasoning often just got in the way. No proof or evidence was needed. When I felt that overwhelming urge to move, to act, to call, to ask, I did it, without question or hesitation. That sixth sense has saved my life a few times!

Leadership lesson #22

We live in a fear-based culture that obsesses over control. We're terrified of uncertainty and vulnerability, forever on guard against the threatening unknown. At the same time, we are under constant pressure to make quick, wise decisions. When the counsel of trusted colleagues is not available, where do we turn? I believe the greatest resource for making sound decisions lies within us.

Call it foresight, words spoken from the heart or a gut feeling, our intuition draws on the accumulation of all our experiences, all the books we have read, all the people we have met, all the insights and facts we have collected throughout our life. Trust your gut. It takes courage to act on a feeling, but your feelings may be your ultimate guidance system.

***

Tune into the elemental energy source, just as the elephants did. It may feel silly at first, but practice heightens your awareness. How often, after poring over all the data and reports, have you fallen back on making a decision based on what your gut tells you? Like courage and optimism, intuition can be cultivated. Start noticing all you can with your five conventional senses. Doing so can raise your sensitivity to your sixth sense.

- Are you too distracted by data, background noise or other people's opinions to tune in to what you 'feel' you should do?

- Have you ever been under such time pressure that the only choice you have is to make a gut decision? How did that work out?

- How often have you felt the conviction that you have to act right now?

Have you cleaned your glasses
recently?

23

Know thyself

How being on lockdown in Pakistan revealed
the power of conditioning

Pleased as I was with what we'd been able to achieve on a practical level in Pakistan, on a personal level I was lonely. The truth was, I was desperate for female companionship. Every day I met only men, whether they were in Armani suits in city boardrooms or grubby *shalwar kameez* in humid villages. I missed women's conversation and the emotional intimacy I could find only in their company. I knew that to help women effectively I needed to walk in their shoes, hear their stories, tap into their lives. I was acutely aware of my limitations: however much I felt I might have succeeded in understanding a situation, on some level I would always be thinking from a European perspective.

I was well into my second year in Pakistan—almost a year after Cyclone Yemyin—before an opportunity arose. I didn't often open the online newsletter for expats that announced forthcoming events, as I was so rarely in town, but this week I happened to be under lockdown in Islamabad, and I felt like a caged animal pacing my apartment. I needed to find something interesting to do, so I scanned the listings without much hope. At that time our movements were so restricted that I guessed most events would be cancelled. Then one item caught my eye: a stress management course at the women's centre. And boy, did I need stress management.

For months now I hadn't been sleeping well. I had got used to living with high levels of tension, but it was taking its toll on my body. A couple of months before, on 15 March 2008, a group of us, journalists and UN security friends, had decided to go out for dinner at a favourite restaurant, the Luna Caprese. We hadn't been out for ages, but there hadn't been a bombing for three months and we thought we would risk it. We had booked a table for 8 pm but were running late. We were a few streets away when we heard an almighty explosion. Minutes later, we received a text on our phones: 'Bomb blast in F6—Luna Caprese Restaurant—situation unknown—AVOID.' Rather than returning home, a couple of us rushed to help. The place was pulverised.

We learned later that the casualties were mostly non-Pakistanis and included a Turkish nurse, seven Americans, a Chinese national, a Briton, a Canadian and two Japanese journalists. That night we steadied our nerves with a bottle of Chivas Regal and for a long time sat in silence, staring into space. There was a sense that the tide had turned and things were going to get a lot worse.

I hoped the stress management course might provide relief, but when I got to the women's centre I thought I must be in the wrong place. The lobby was packed with jostling men. Then I remembered that if you were a woman in Pakistan, a male member of the family had to accompany you to a venue and stay until you left.

Adding my purple ankle boots to the pile of ladies' shoes left outside the hall I pushed open the swing door and entered. The room was large. Cushioned mats lay scattered about the floor. The curtains were drawn—to keep out men's prying eyes, I guessed. Candles flickered from the stage, the scent of jasmine filled the room. Music played quietly in the background. I looked around me hoping to make eye contact with someone. I was the only foreigner. The other women were mostly wearing *burkhas* and *hijabs* so it was difficult to guess their age. A few sat in pairs, heads close together, whispering. Most of them sat quietly, eyes down, lost in their own world. I found a mat near the back and got out my notepad and pen.

A few moments later, our teacher breezed in. She had an energy about her that was enchanting. The group followed her every movement, spellbound. Pakistani ladies almost always keep their black hair long, tied back in a severe ponytail. Hers was short and wavy, a light-brown bob that bounced as she walked. She was wearing a white cotton full-length dress with a shawl around her shoulders, embroidered with pink roses. Amongst the black *burkhas* the contrast was striking. She looked like an angel.

She stood with arms wide open and spoke in a warm, low voice. 'Welcome ladies, and thank you for coming. My name is Jeannie.' She introduced our session by acknowledging how hard it must have been for many of the group to come. 'Weeks of gentle persuasion at home ... our menfolk are very protective of us, yes? So ...' She sought their eyes. 'Well done. I applaud you. You did it, and now you are here!'

She told us that in this room we were sisters, that there was no need for shyness or fear.

'Anything that is said in this room is confidential. It will not be repeated to anyone. This is a rule. We must have absolute trust.' Jeannie scanned the room, looking into our eyes, extracting a silent promise from each of us. Once she was satisfied, her serious expression fell away and her playfulness returned. She asked us to give our names, one by one, and say a little about ourselves. She suggested I go first. 'I would like us all to welcome Linda, a guest from our foreign community. It is so nice to have you with us.'

Twenty pairs of eyes gazed at me. I couldn't read their expression.

Words tumbled out. '*Assalam aleikum*. My name is Linda. I am a social worker from England. I have been living and working in Pakistan for over a year. With the recent bomb blasts I can't get to my projects in Sindh. I have come here to relax and make new friends.'

One by one the women were called upon to introduce themselves. Silence hung heavy in the room following each intense outpouring.

Priya, from Rawalpindi, spoke next, explaining that her husband was a bully and her in-laws wanted her to give up her job in the bank. 'I have no freedom...I just want to die.'

This is not going to be a light relaxation class, I thought, as Priya started to sob quietly.

'Thank you, Priya,' Jeannie said tenderly. 'And can you tell us what you hope to gain from the course?'

Priya swallowed her tears with difficulty. 'I want to learn how to survive my situation.'

Priya's honesty encouraged other women to open up. One by one, bursting with pent-up anger and bitterness, they shared their stories. These were women who were sufficiently well-off to pay the course fees, but their lives had many of the same restrictions as those of the villagers I had encountered.

Thirty-year-old Nida, desperate for a divorce, spoke of eight years of hell. 'I am being suffocated day by day,' she said. 'I do not believe this is the life Allah wants for me!' When she was asked what she wanted to get from the course, she spoke passionately: 'Courage not to give up. Strength and encouragement from other women, who know what it is like to suffer every day.'

I was shocked by the burden of pain each of the women was carrying. I thought of the men waiting in the lobby. *Their ears must be burning.*

The introductions completed, Jeannie asked us to get to our feet and find a space. 'Time to get your bodies moving!'

She asked us to breathe deeply, to feel the music in our bodies. Knowing many of us would feel self-conscious, she suggested we keep our eyes closed. I began to move to the music, dropping my shoulders, feeling my body grow lighter as the tension ebbed away. I hadn't danced like this since those wonderful evenings at the Marley Café in Thailand. After a little, I ventured a peep at the other women, curious to know if they were joining in. It was a surreal and beautiful sight. They had thrown themselves into the dance with abandon. *Burkhas* were whipping round and billowing like the robes of whirling dervishes. Hips were swaying, arms moving as expressively as in a Hawaiian hula dance. It spoke of a feeling of safety. Of liberation. Of birds escaping their cages and flying free.

Afterwards, there was clapping and laughter, an exchange of smiles. Then, as we lined up at the water dispenser, I was brought sharply back to earth.

'You hate us!' A woman, in front of me in the line, almost spat out the words.

'Sorry?' I said, completely taken aback.

'What are you doing here? Are you a spy?' she asked, eyes narrowed. 'The mullah comes to our university most days. He tells us. He knows.'

'He knows what?' I said indignantly.

'You have no respect for us.'

'Would I be here if I felt like that? It's dangerous for me. I'm risking my life here.' Tears welled in my eyes.

The girl glared at me, silent. I took a breath, decided to change the subject. I asked her what she was studying at university. She told me she was a medic. Then her frustrations came pouring out. I guess she had decided I wasn't a spy after all.

'It's a waste of time. When my parents find me a husband he will never let me have a job,' she said bitterly. 'It's a joke.'

Jeannie called us together again. This time she wanted us to sit cross-legged facing a partner. It was an exercise in love, she told us. The love that connects each one of us, every second of every day.

A feeling of unease once again filled the room. 'I don't know anything about love,' one of the youngest girls said. 'I can't do this.'

'Yes you can,' said Jeannie. 'Just think of a newborn baby in your arms. What would you feel then?'

'Love,' the girl replied reluctantly.

'Please take your partner's hands and look into her eyes. That is all I want you to do. Don't talk. Just look into her eyes,' Jeannie said. 'Get comfortable. You'll be doing this for ten minutes.'

My partner's hands were calloused. She had dark circles under her eyes. At first, we were both embarrassed to look at each other. We glanced sideways, up and down, anywhere but straight ahead. Many of the women shuffled around or giggled nervously. Jeannie asked for quiet.

Then the magic began. Our inhibitions fell away and we did as we were told, imagining the word *love*, the essence of love, in our mind's eye. I felt a connection with my partner that went way beyond the physical, breaking through the barriers. We were merely two human beings connecting, soul to soul.

'Now drop your hands,' Jeannie said. I couldn't believe ten minutes had passed already. 'If you feel like it, you can give each other a hug.' All of us hugged and most of us wept a few tears as well. 'You are never alone,' Jeannie said quietly. 'All you have to do is look into someone's eyes. Then you don't see strangers around you. You see friends.'

We finished the session doing shoulder stands. As the women raised their legs in the air, their *burkhas* tumbled over their heads. Everyone was giggling.

Later, when I was sifting through the piles of shoes to find mine, I felt a light tap on my shoulder. It was the medical student. 'Sorry,' she said. 'I know what I said isn't true. Do you think we could meet up for a cup of coffee?' We hugged and exchanged phone numbers. 'Do you know much about Islam, Linda?' she asked. I shook my head. 'Not much. Only a little.'

She dug into her bag and brought out a book. 'Please accept this gift,' she said shyly.

I stammered my thanks.

'It's an English translation of the Koran,' she said. 'I would like you to have it.'

I walked out into the cool night air and watched while the men bundled their women hurriedly into waiting cars.

'Did you have a good evening, madam?' Faisal was holding open the car door.

'I did, thank you, Faisal.'

Faisal beamed and gave me a double thumbs-up, a gesture he had caught off me.

Leadership lesson #23

Every culture has rules and values its citizens take for granted. These tend to be based on the beliefs, conditioning, anxieties and expectations we absorb from the society of which we are a part. Few of us are aware of the filters through which we view the world, because cultural imprinting begins at a very early age and happens without conscious thought.

A pivotal part of being a great leader is understanding, and helping others gain awareness of, the filters through which we perceive the world. Reach for those deep-seated fears inside yourself. If you find yourself answering a question reflexively, ask it again. Challenge yourself when you feel you could be stuck in conditioned thinking.

***

When you jump to a conclusion, question yourself. Why do you think that? Whose rules are you living by? Your reality is filtered through your beliefs. Notice your shoulds and oughts, as they will often signal old conditioning.

- What assumptions, judgements and deep-seated opinions do you bring to the workplace?

- What is important to you? What would you risk your life for?

- What do you stand for, and what won't you stand for?

Post earthquake, Pakistan

Have you ever stayed too long
in a toxic environment?

24

Know when to leave

How I was torn between staying and leaving Pakistan in the midst of terrorism

In the two years I lived and worked in Pakistan I saw the havoc wreaked by numerous suicide bombers. Some cities, like Karachi, were almost completely out of bounds. I was based in Islamabad, which was slightly safer, but anxiety about terrorist attacks still peppered our conversation. Even charity workers were at risk. Rumour had it that many of them were CIA operatives. Some undoubtedly were; they usually stood out a mile in their perfectly pressed *shalwar kameez*. In some people's minds, we were all potential spies, so every aid worker's life was in danger.

Embassies pared down their staff and sent the families of their employees home. They had set up a useful warning system. Whenever there was a gunman or bomber on the loose, or even word of a protest, we were alerted immediately by text message. Every day we were sent messages to be vigilant, with reminders to avoid shopping centres, mosques, restaurants, hotels or the diplomatic enclave where the embassies were situated. Living in a state of high alert was new to me, but I swiftly learned to sense the mood, to feel an atmosphere, to sense potential danger. We clutched our mobile phones everywhere we went, anticipating the worst.

Then, on 22 September 2008, the Marriott Hotel was bombed.

It was the final straw for many of us. The hotel had been thought to be impregnable, its security second to none. In the hotel's plush interior we could relax, forgetting for a short while what was happening on the other side of the walls.

The blast was the biggest Pakistan had ever seen. Every one of the Marriott's 290 rooms was gutted by fire. The bomb left a huge crater and a death toll of 53.

The writing had been on the wall ever since Benazir Bhutto's assassination the previous December. I had escaped death a few times. I didn't know how much longer my luck would hold. It was time to leave, and I knew it. The most important thing was not to become complacent or predictable. A great friend of mine had been kidnapped two days before he was due to leave his posting. He had dropped his guard, talked loosely. Who knows? Without telling anyone, I bought a one-way ticket to London and left.

Back home in England, I found it difficult to adjust. I kept looking at people, especially women, going about their everyday lives with a freedom they took completely for granted. My first day home, I headed out to the shopping mall. Delighted not to have to wear a *hijab*, and free to do whatever I pleased, I felt relaxed for the first time in ages. I was in the pharmacist's browsing at the cosmetics counter.

Suddenly there was a loud crash behind me. I threw myself under the counter, my hands over my head. Where I'd just come from, if you waited a split second to confirm the source of a noise like that, the next one might get you. There was no second bang. Just the voice of a kindly shop assistant.

'Can I help you?' The woman was looking down at me with concern. 'Are you all right?'

I could hear her voice but I dared not move.

A hand gently touched my shoulder and I flinched. 'It's just one of our delivery trucks.'

She helped me to my feet. I was embarrassed to find that a crowd of curious onlookers had gathered.

'I'm sorry. I've … just come from Pakistan. I thought …'

'Can I get you some water?' the woman asked.

'No.' I smiled to reassure her. 'I'm fine now.' I hurried away, my knees still shaking from the shock. I could feel the cool rain but did not notice how wet I was getting. I just needed to walk.

The experience of Pakistan has never left me. To this day when I enter a hotel room, I move the bed away from the window and draw the curtains. Some reflexes are simply hardwired in me now. It was a difficult time—an ugly time in many ways—but I wouldn't have swapped a minute of it. I still live life on the edge and regularly take risks, but since Pakistan my appreciation of life, of human rights, is much greater. I savour the freedom I have, knowing that millions have never known it.

Pakistan taught me some of the most important lessons of my life.

Leadership lesson #24

You spend two-thirds of your life at work. Do you feel energised by the experience or simply drained? The stress of working in a dysfunctional office, undermined by bad attitudes, poor communication, bullying or a tyrannical boss, can carry over into your personal life, damaging everything from your self-esteem to your friendships and health. Don't waste your life. A short bad relationship is better than a long bad relationship. How do you want to be remembered?

***

Some circumstances and events will be beyond your control. There will probably be times when you know you have the capacity to contribute more intellectually or emotionally, but because of your need for financial security, or perhaps your ambition, you find yourself locked in a toxic work environment long after you know you should move on.

- Do you recognise this syndrome?

- Have you found you have exhausted your toolkit of skills and resources and need to let go?

- What can you leave or let go of in your role that is creating unreasonable stress for you?

Post cyclone and flood, Pakistan

When did you last form
a judgement based on
assumptions rather than true
understanding?

25

Do not judge

How racism gave way to compassion in a Burmese refugee camp in Thailand

As I walked into the lobby of the gleaming tower block in Bangkok that housed Manpower's offices, I wondered how Simon's staff would cope in the mud and squalor of the refugee camps. It was beautifully cool inside. There was a small coffee shop just inside the entrance where smartly dressed office workers were sipping cappuccinos and chatting. I took a lift to the first floor and walked through the automatic glass doors. Inside, all was quiet efficiency, hushed and carpeted, a relief from the buzz and bustle of the busy city streets. An organised, high-tech world of computers, multimedia projectors and whiteboards. Rows of gleaming white tables and chairs in bright, vibrant colours to inspire the team creatively.

The receptionist beamed at me. 'Linda, we've been expecting you. Let me show you to the meeting room.'

A minute later, staff members began to gather in the room. They were young and fashionably dressed, the men in pastel shirts with contrasting ties, the women in pretty summer dresses and high heels. They brought with them a whiff of expensive aftershave and perfume.

Simon strode in with a cheerful *'Sawadee ka!'* to everyone, then shook my hand warmly. 'What a great turnout. I'm delighted!'

After introducing me, Simon asked if any of them could tell him what Manpower's four pillars of social responsibility were. Eee, the marketing manager, called out from the back of the room.

'Workforce development. Disaster recovery. Reaching out to refugees. Combating human trafficking.'

'Correct,' said Simon. 'And this project will come under reaching out to refugees.'

Simon had warned me we'd have our work cut out to gather a team. Because of the difficult economic times, they would only be able to work on the project outside office hours. It was an incredible commitment. Many of them already worked a 12-hour day, and now we were asking them to give up precious hours of their weekends. We weren't going to strong-arm anyone. If the project was to work, it needed a group prepared to make a commitment for a decent period. It needed enthusiasm as well as persistence. It's true what they say: 'One volunteer is worth ten pressed men'.

Simon reminded the group of one of Manpower's main mission statements: *to connect an individual to the dignity and independence of work.* This is of particular relevance to the refugees, who were not permitted to work inside or outside the camps.

Burma has been a military dictatorship since 1962. Many of the refugees who fled to the refugee camps over the Thai border are Karen, an ethnic group that has long experienced a myriad human rights violations, including torture, rape and forced labour. Most crossed the border, seeded with landmines, only when they had exhausted all other options. They are unwilling guests, hating that they've been forced to leave their country. Patriotic, they fight to retain their own identity, customs and religion.

The refugees have come to form a significant minority in Thailand, where they are widely condemned as lazy and dependent on handouts or accused of taking locals' jobs. About 150 000 live in nine camps, Mae Sot being the largest. Some have lived there for more than 20 years. As Thai law forbids refugee labour, only by going 'under the wire' and working illegally outside the camp can they supplement the inadequate camp rations. So it is that there is a willing pool of 80 000 underpaid and exploited migrant workers in the Mae Sot region alone, where factory owners see no need to pay minimum wage or provide acceptable working conditions.

After Simon had described the refugee situation briefly, he handed over to me. I sensed the mood had dipped so I decided to throw out some questions and make the presentation more interactive. However powerfully Simon had introduced the project, his staff were yet to be convinced to give up their free time to work with people they neither trusted nor liked.

'What are you going to do today when you leave the office?' I asked. 'Chirawat, you start.'

Chirawat grinned at the group. He was an extrovert and a sharp dresser. 'I'm going to the mall to buy some sports shoes.' One of his friends gave a wolf whistle.

I went quickly round the group. 'Going to the movies'…'Seeing my boyfriend' (another whoop from the crowd)…'Planning my holiday'…'Playing on the internet.'

'Do you feel safe when you're doing these things?' I asked them.

'Of course!' came the chorus of replies.

I asked them what they knew of the Burmese.

'My family always have Burmese maids,' a young woman said.

'And how's that been?' I asked.

She shrugged. 'Some are great, like they're part of the family. Some unreliable…steal, disappear without warning.'

There were sounds of agreement from the group. I asked another what he knew of the refugees.

'They're cheap labour,' he said. 'I see it all the time at work. We try and place Thai people in a company and find it's full of illegal Burmese. Being paid half the salary. It's not right.'

'But why are the Burmese here? Why aren't they at home in their country?' I asked, scanning the room.

'Better conditions here,' one of the group spoke up. 'Life is easy.'

'All true,' I said.

Simon caught my eye, knowing I was on sensitive ground, encouraging me to go on. I told the group that I was going to show them three pictures I had taken during my first visit to the Mae Sot camp the previous week. I paused while they absorbed them—the cramped living conditions, the sea of mud.

'Can you imagine being born there, and never knowing any of the freedoms you enjoy? No trips to the mall? No popping into the supermarket to buy your favourite snack? No chance to use the internet or watch TV?

'There's an old saying: Before you judge a man, walk a mile in his moccasins,' I went on. 'Close your eyes for a moment. Imagine you are a Burmese refugee. Wear their shoes. See how it feels.'

Four months earlier, in October 2008, I had made my first visit to Mae Sot. I was still over an hour's drive from the Burmese border when my car was stopped at a heavily armed military checkpoint, an elaborate affair of barriers and barbed wire. It was to be the first of many. I had never seen such a high level of security around refugees. Sniffer dogs with their handlers patrolled the cars, which were searched thoroughly, every bag opened and scrutinised. The line stretched out in each direction.

'What are they looking for?' I asked my driver.

'Stowaways, weapons, drugs,' he said. 'Much illegal traffic on this border. Army very busy.'

I looked at the powerful spotlights and cameras surrounding the interrogation area. The driver read my thoughts.

'They don't come through in cars,' he said. 'The jungle is very thick. Easy to hide. Many snakes.'

I shuddered, looking out at the lush jungle on either side of the road, the plants and trees on an epic scale. It was like something out of *Jurassic Park*. We set off again and I held my breath as we climbed steep hills and hurtled down the other side despite hairpin bends, blind corners and sheer descents. The driver drove fast, overtaking struggling lorries that belched out great clouds of black smoke on the hill climbs. I was relieved when we finally drew up outside the offices of ZOA, the charity with which Manpower proposed to team up.

I was met by Ka, one of the key people at ZOA. I warmed to him immediately. He was a handsome man in his thirties, with soft features that looked more Tibetan or Mongolian than Thai. It turned out he was Karen Burmese, married to a Thai woman. I quickly came to see what an asset he was to the charity, especially given his fluency in Karen as well as Thai and English.

He led me to his jeep. 'Your permit is only for today,' he said. 'No time to waste, I'm afraid.'

It was an hour's drive to Mae La camp, the largest of the seven camps dotted along the border. Ka briefed me on the way. 'We get a lot of flare-ups along the border between the ethnic armies and the military,' he told me. 'Mae La is only 8 kilometres from Burma.' He told me that any minute now I might catch a glimpse of the notorious Thahan Phran, or Black Rangers, a combat-hardened military border force whose name means 'hunter soldiers'.

'It's a very porous border,' Ka explained. 'We get new arrivals most days, many of them injured by landmines.'

We talked of the resettlement program and I asked him, 'Don't you think it will only serve to sweep the refugee problem under the carpet? It doesn't exactly keep up the pressure on the Thai government and Burmese junta to work out a solution nearer to home.'

'Certainly a valid point,' he said. 'It's not going to help the democracy movement if the resistance to the junta is taken away.' He then explained one of the most pressing problems in the camps. Certain Western nations, including Finland and Canada, would only take in the more educated and skilled refugees. As a result of this brain drain, there were few teachers or medics left to work in the camps. 'We've got as many as 20 000 uneducated refugees, without language or local knowledge, being dumped in the States with little support,' he said. 'That's where we need help.'

'So you're hoping Manpower staff can create an education package?' I asked.

'What teachers we have don't have the skills. They're barely trained,' Ka said. 'This needs to be efficient. We only get three or four weeks' warning when a refugee's name comes up.'

I had heard some of the stories. The Karen people had no idea how to perform the most basic tasks in their new country. They had no notion of saving money, having always lived on a hand-to-mouth basis. Western notions of timekeeping were a mystery to them, which had proved a problem with employers.

'Even on the plane on the way to New York they get into difficulties,' Ka said wryly. 'They worry that they will have to pay to use the toilet. So they hold on, the whole flight. One older woman collapsed.'

My mind boggled as I tried to imagine the refugees, one day in a jungle war zone, the next in an urban metropolis. 'Culture shock' doesn't come near to describing it. Things would have to change.

After driving for an hour, the jeep rounded a bend and there it was, nestled at the base of a beautiful green mountain. An endless floating canopy of overlapping sun-dried brown leaves, crisp and curled up at the edges: the roofs of the camp dwellings. They lined the roadside right up to the wire fence marking the camp boundary. We passed small groups of children behind the fence, jumping up and down and waving. After one last checkpoint, we were through the high iron gate of the camp's main entrance.

Ka jumped out of the jeep and went over to report in at the camp commander's office. Ka had told me that foreigners, even those working for the aid agencies, were forbidden to stay overnight at the camp, so I would have to be signed out by nightfall.

He got back into the car. 'Apparently there were some gang fights last night,' he said. 'They are a bit twitchy. Scared you might be a journalist. The army hates to lose face.'

I asked Ka what the gang fighting was about. He told me it was an increasing problem, with 65 per cent of the camp population under 25 years of age.

'You can imagine what happens,' he said. 'All that boredom and lack of hope. Fighting is a release. They pick on the new arrivals. Easy prey.'

We drove down a rough dirt road lined with deep, muddy furrows. The brakes groaned as the jeep slid its way down the hill.

'Lucky you've got four-wheel drive,' I said.

'One of our jeeps got stuck here last year. We had to get an elephant to pull it out. Very embarrassing!'

The mud was all-pervasive. It stained the bodies of everyone living in the camp. At a water pump, rows of buckets were waiting to be filled and taken back to the little shelters built on stilts. I doubted the women bothered to wash their children—they'd be fighting a losing battle.

We pulled up outside the camp leader's house. As I picked my way carefully to the steps, I was touched to see that they had made me a welcome sign, which was hanging on the porch: 'A warm and hearty welcome to Linda Cruse.' Standing in front of it was the camp leader, Dee, a short, stout man with receding grey hair. He greeted me warmly. I added my shoes to a mountain of muddy flip-flops at the doorway and went through.

Inside, the Camp Committee were sitting cross-legged on the bamboo floor, each wearing the traditional Karen red-and-blue woven shirt or tunic, a matching woven shoulder bag, containing their most treasured possessions, on their laps. I joined them and we spoke of the main issues affecting the camp.

One unforeseen problem that had emerged in recent months was that the influx of aid money from overseas and the resettlement program had drawn the poor from other communities to the camps. Many Bangladeshis and Indians had made their way through Burma on foot in the hope of being resettled.

'It's one of the reasons the refugees are not allowed to work,' Dee told me. 'The government doesn't want to encourage more of them to cross the border.'

Ka had already touched on the sensitive political situation with Burma, made more so by the presence of the refugee camps. Thailand had to play a careful game if it was to preserve its relationship with Burma, an important trading neighbour. Burma is a country rich in mineral deposits, natural gas and timber. Some nations—Russia and China especially—compete for these commodities, while others favour a boycott, outraged by the military junta's brutal suppression of democracy.

We didn't stay long. Soon I was being taken on a tour of the camp. Everywhere we went the story was the same. No work, low self-esteem, and boredom that spread like a deadly virus, infecting everyone, especially the young people. Parents worried about their children. One woman described the sex trafficking that was rife in the border area. She said the Thai and Burmese drug lords were becoming richer and more powerful by the day, growing opium and churning out methamphetamines. She feared for her teenage daughter. So many girls, with little to keep them in the camps, were being lured into sex work.

I met some of the students at the community centre. Ka told me to be prepared for a bombardment of questions: 'Time is one thing they have way too much of.'

Ka was greeted by friendly boos and a football thrown directly at his chest. There were about twenty students in the centre. He took me over to meet one of them, a boy of 16, with dyed red hair and elaborate tattoos.

'Linda, this is Idy,' Ka said, patting the boy on the shoulder before disappearing to the back of the room to see how the food was coming along.

'I love your tattoos,' I said to him.

'The monks gave them to me, for protection,' he said. 'I move around a lot so I need it.'

I asked Idy how he'd come to be here. He told me he was the oldest boy in the family. His father had been killed by a landmine while trying to reach the camp. It was up to him to provide for the family now. They couldn't survive on camp rations so he had to go under the wire and earn some extra money in town.

A boy in a red bandana with an angry knife wound on his cheek, who was sitting next to Idy, said, 'If they catch him, he'll be sent back over the border.'

'The Thais know it, so they do what they like to us,' Idy said. 'I had one boss, didn't give me anything on pay day. Said if I made a fuss he'd report me.'

He told me they were offered vocational training in the camps: weaving, stove making, basket weaving, car mechanics, haircutting, cooking.

He finished the paper aeroplane he had been making and launched it into the air. 'It keeps us busy. But for what? Most of us don't bother to go any more.'

I could see his point. Khun Ka was right. Resettlement was the best option these young people had. Otherwise it was a downward spiral.

As if he knew I would need to see something uplifting before the day came to a close, Ka had left the best for last. A pilot project, funded by ZOA, it allowed a group of refugees to work outside the camp. Ka was hugely heartened by its success.

'Come, I'll show you. It's a small farm, just one plot of land at this stage. Across the road from the camp. It's amazing. Only a few steps away, but it's given them such a morale boost, leaving the camp to go to work.'

We signed out and left the camp. I followed Ka up a steep dirt track to where a small group of men were sitting under a tree. They were painfully thin. Ka told me they were all blind. Three of them were missing limbs and wore old-fashioned prostheses, flesh-coloured above the ankle, but black feet with mock toes below. It looked sinister, as though the foot was rotting. But what seemed strangest of all, considering what poor shape they were in, was the joking, laughing and sheer joy they exuded. They called out to us as we approached. Ka introduced me.

One of the group, a man missing most of his fingers, said to Ka, 'Take her to see our work. We've cleared a big patch, ready for planting tomorrow.'

Ka joked with him, and all the men laughed uproariously. Once we had walked on and were out of earshot, I asked what had happened to the man.

'That's Saw,' he said. 'Amazing man. Former freedom fighter. He was tortured. They chopped off his fingers. That was before a landmine blew off his leg and blinded him.'

'I can't get over how happy they seem.'

'They love the project. It's given them a purpose,' he said. 'They're great workers.'

We climbed further up the steep dirt slope until we had a view of the whole area. A large chunk of the hillside had been cultivated.

'Over there is the frog farm where we harvest the legs for sale to restaurants,' Ka pointed to two big concrete tanks. 'And in the shed there, we've started a mushroom farm. A high-value crop. We're hoping it will fund a lot of new projects.'

'How many have you got working here?' I asked.

'A hundred and sixty,' he said. 'We've chosen them carefully. Women-headed households, the disabled and sexually vulnerable. We've allowed them to choose what they grow.'

This was music to my ears.

'The latest new business idea is to grow flowers,' he said. 'It's been brilliant. They're selling them in the camps for weddings, funerals and birthdays.'

The success of the flower business had fired up the refugees. Now they were asking to set up worm farms and beehives; and they wanted to plant more high-value vegetables. A true sign of the success of the project was that 27 of the initial 80 who started the project saved their 1800 baht per month salary given by ZOA and went on to invest it in their own business within the camp. Their latest initiative was chilli growing.

'The aid agencies could no longer afford to give them chillies, so guess what—they're growing their own!'

We walked into a small office and sat near a fan. Ka took a couple of cans from the fridge and we drank thirstily.

'In January we had the first sign of growth from the land,' he said, clapping his hands together, delighting in the memory. 'Our greatest joy was to hear the refugees singing in the fields.'

ZOA had been careful not to step on the toes of the Thai locals, many of whom are very poor. The charity did not want to create any more animosity or jealousy than there already was, so the pilot project outside the camp involved both Burmese and Thais.

Dissolving barriers between the two races, both fiercely patriotic, with many reasons not to like each other, would be an important factor in the Manpower project. We would be bringing together rich city kids and traumatised rural farmers, and the only way we could bridge the gap of distrust that divided them was to have them meet, face to face. Simon had been certain that his staff, who had been under huge pressure of late to deliver in a tough economic market, would benefit from the diversion that this charitable project offered. He was right.

Twenty-five Manpower employees signed up. Of those, Simon and I selected four team leaders whom we would take on an insight trip to

Mae Sot. Once they had met the refugees they would be helping, their objective was to work out a plan in line with their mission statement, which was: *'To equip refugees with skills necessary to become socially and economically successful citizens in resettlement countries'.*

The four team leaders were nervous at first, concerned that they wouldn't be able to communicate and that the refugees might be hostile to them. I assured them this would not be the case.

'Just be open-minded. Ask questions and then listen without judging. You may not agree with all you hear. Allow them to share their fears, their hopes, their dreams. Get to know them as people. See where they live, what they do, how they feel.'

At Mae La camp, the group was taken first to an English language class. The teacher asked them if they would like to sing an ABBA song the Burmese students were learning. For a moment, I saw the team hesitate, looking at each other, embarrassed. Then a painfully thin Karen boy took Chanarat's arm, encouraging him to get to his feet and to join in. Soon we were all standing in a tight group, singing our hearts out.

Deeply emotional stories were shared. Stories that melted any unfounded resentment. I saw a tear trickle down Khun Chirawat's cheek as he listened to a young Burmese man share how he was forced to witness his brother being beaten to death. They were no longer enemies but brothers sharing the pain.

UNHCR (United Nations High Commissioner for Refugees) were impressed with the energy shown by the Manpower volunteers. It was agreed that, in partnership with ZOA and IOM (International Organization for Migration), the volunteers would redesign IOM's current 25-hour orientation program, including the English language skills component, and also develop a three-week to three-month curriculum, based on ZOA's current English language curriculum. For the pilot, 50 refugees would be selected, from the thousand who had been formally approved and selected for resettlement to the United States but had not yet been given a departure date. Of that number, an initial group of 15 would be trained.

Once we had listed the main issues—high teacher turnover, teaching methods, teacher quality, and lack of teaching aids and illustrations—the team set about creating standardised curriculum and lesson plans that any new teacher could pick up and run with, and teaching materials, including scrapbooks of pictures and flashcards. They had witnessed Burmese students learning by rote, and devised a new set of interactive, fun activities that would help them retain information more effectively.

My job was done. I was confident that my small group of four had everything they needed to empower their own teams, which, in turn, would teach a new group—Burmese this time—to be camp trainers. The process spread like wildfire, as did the goodwill and understanding between two groups of people who had formerly shared only mutual suspicion.

Leadership lesson #25

We judge people all the time. It's hardwired in us. Right now you are probably thinking, 'Was this worth reading? Will it help me develop my leadership?' So why are we so ready to judge others? Is it from fear, or insecurity, or even shame? We cannot know the pain, joy, worries and fears of others unless we take the time to understand them. 'Want to help someone?' asks Ernesto Sirolli. 'Shut up and listen!'

Leaders are paid for their judgement, but when we judge and label others, we deny ourselves the trust and connection that is essential to leadership. As a leader, first take responsibility for yourself. Why have you formed this opinion? What is it based on? Is it valid? When you have put your own house in order, you have greater clarity to lead others.

***

Take a look at yourself in the mirror. Do you think people would know everything (even *anything*) about you from looking at you for five minutes? Probably not. Think of a situation in which you reached a judgement about a person or situation based on unwarranted assumptions. Judging others can often feel awkward, mainly because we ourselves don't like to be judged.

- When is judgement of others useful, and when does it go wrong?

- Do you take time to ask questions before proceeding to judgement, approaching others for their opinions and insights?

- When you misjudge, how easy do you find it to admit your mistake?

Epilogue
Passion, purpose and playfulness

In November 2013, I had just returned to my hotel in Santa Barbara, California, following a long day presenting at a major conference. I went up to my room, threw my bag onto the bed and switched on the TV, hoping to catch up on world news and unwind a little. A sombre news anchor appeared on screen against a backdrop of horrific images of devastation in the Philippines. The presenter explained that a super-typhoon had hit the country's eastern seaboard a few hours earlier and caused widespread death and destruction. For a long time I sat on the edge of the bed, transfixed by the reports on what would turn out to be one of the most powerful storms on record.

The thirtieth major storm in the season, Typhoon Haiyan began a few days before as an area of low pressure in Micronesia. Gradually building in strength, it made landfall in China, Taiwan and Vietnam, but the greatest impact would be in the Philippines, where the storm killed more than 6000 people and made many more homeless. A national emergency was declared, but given the extent of the devastation this had little immediate effect. For several weeks, many thousands of people remained in desperate need of food, shelter and medical assistance. Widespread destruction of the country's infrastructure hampered the relief efforts of the major aid agencies. Emergency rations and aid would not reach countless rural communities for several more months.

Although the instinct to get on the first plane was overwhelming, I knew my skills and experience would be put to better use in the recovery phase. I finally touched down in Manila in January 2014, six weeks after the storm. Before I left the United States, a friend had put me in touch with a relative of hers, Father Robbie, a local priest based on Iloilo Island. I soon learned that his village had been devastated, literally torn to pieces. He confirmed my fears that most of the aid had gone to the epicentre, the city of Tacloban, leaving remote areas without help.

As you'll have gathered from earlier stories, my goal has always been to seek out forgotten villages, off the beaten track, far from airports, cities or good communication. The village of Carles fitted the profile perfectly and I asked Father Robbie for his help in getting there. Before the storm, Carles was a typical local fishing village in the north-east of Iloilo Island, an area renowned for its fishing, corn, sugar, cattle, bakeries, shell craft and wooden furniture. I landed in the capital, Iloilo City, where I met Father Robbie. A few days later I set off on the five-hour journey by minibus to Carles, arriving after dark at the area's only surviving bed and breakfast.

Entering the village, it was a relief to get out of the bus and stretch my legs, but my relief was short-lived. Everywhere I looked, families were sitting in or picking through the ruins of their shattered homes. The streets that crisscrossed the village were lined with battered, bare palm trees stripped of their foliage, that seemed to embody the sense of hopelessness I saw in people's faces. I walked down to the sea. The beach was strewn with debris; shards of houses, trees and fishing boats reduced to splinters and thrown about like confetti. A local guide told us that further down the coast a power-barge had been driven ashore. The wreck was slowly and steadily poisoning the sea with oil, a final fatal blow for this fishing community.

Almost all the fishermen had seen their livelihoods destroyed the day the storm picked up their boats and dropped them inland in a thousand pieces. Once proud breadwinners, the men were now unable to provide for their families and watched helplessly as their children slowly starved. In a cruel irony, those lucky enough to own one of the few fishing vessels to survive the catastrophe could no longer fish in the contaminated water.

When I arrive on the frontline of a natural disaster, I can never be sure what I'll find. It was ten weeks since the typhoon struck and 90 per cent of the families of Carles still had no shelter to speak of. Electricity pylons hung down at precarious angles and debris covered every surface. Mercifully, local church people had brought food to the village as soon as the road was cleared, but these supplies were rapidly dwindling and further help had yet to arrive.

What I found in Carles was worse than I had feared. Out of 592 households, 457 had lost everything, including their homes and livelihoods. I was all too conscious of the enormity of my task. In the coming days I was introduced to one of the village's trusted leaders. Ramil Pancho wasn't an elected leader, but he was respected, loved and admired by everyone. He would prove to be a wonderful ally.

In the following days, Ramil and I walked through the village, introducing ourselves, meeting families and assessing their needs. Even this brought hope to the faces of the mothers. I began to spend time with individual families, sitting with them, learning what they had been through. For fathers, who had tried so hard to remain strong for their families, a kind word or touch now could unman them so that they would crumple, unable to speak. Despite what they had been through, the survivors greeted us with smiles and embraces, many offering to share the little food they had.

In some parts of the village the atmosphere was tense, and emotions were raw. I saw teenagers who would normally be full of fun and laughter sobbing uncontrollably and younger children lying listlessly in the laps of their broken, hopeless parents. Every day, more tears.

Sitting down with families, it was humbling to learn of their courage on the day of the typhoon. The same story over and over: the terrible noise, the rising water, nowhere to shelter from the terrifying onslaught, falling to the ground, crawling on hands and knees to find refuge, clutching at children and loved ones, crouching under a table or kneeling against a wall, not daring to move for fear of being struck by flying sheets of roofing iron. And after, no food, no water, no home, no hope.

Prioritising families, deciding who to help first, knowing they are all in such need, is always painfully difficult. Drawing on my frontline experience, I enlisted teachers and village leaders to help identify the women and children most at risk. Word spread that I had a medical background, so patients arrived in a steady stream that threatened to overwhelm my main work.

Each evening I arrived back at base dirty, exhausted, covered in mosquito bites and nursing an upset stomach (maybe too many flies got to the food first), but determined to make an even earlier start the next day.

Then I met Mary Ann Candelona for the first time. Mary Ann lives a long way from the village on a little land owned by her family. We arrived in a small two-seater *tuk-tuk*, wending our way down narrow dirt tracks flanked by fields of towering sugarcane. Mary Ann's home had been badly damaged, and she was now living with her four children in a makeshift bamboo shelter. We found her sitting motionless, clutching her newborn tightly to her chest. It was immediately apparent that Mary Ann was severely traumatised. It was as though she was emotionally frozen, simply lacking the will to go on. She didn't even respond to our arrival. Ramil was the first to speak. Crouching down beside her, he explained why we were there. She responded by repeating the word 'salamat' (thank you) in almost a whisper. I looked around the shelter. I could see no food or cooking utensils and wondered how she and her children were surviving.

After that meeting, we struggled to think of ways to give Mary Ann an economic hand up that could be sustainable and allow her to remain at home for her children. When the typhoon struck, Mary Ann was 34 years old and eight months pregnant. She, her husband and their three other children had made their way to her mother's home, where they all crawled under a bed. The typhoon was much worse than they had expected, and as the house began to peel away around them Mary Ann was terrified she would give birth prematurely. They knew the house wouldn't last much longer and now offered negligible shelter, so they fled outside and huddled under a large tree as the wind screamed around them and sent debris flying past their heads.

Once the worst of the storm had passed, the family were left with nothing but the clothes they were wearing. 'It was so dark, I thought it was the end of the world. After the hurricane, we had nothing — we were completely helpless.'

They had survived, but their nightmare wasn't over. Within a few weeks, as they faced the daunting task of rebuilding their shattered home, Mary Ann gave birth to her fourth child. It should have been a joyful occasion, but very soon afterwards her husband was killed in a motorcycle accident.

Even in the depths of her grief, Mary Ann knew she had to carry on for the sake of her children, but she had no idea how she could support them.

By the time we arrived, Mary Ann and her family were beginning to starve. No one was able to lend her money and the children were no longer attending school. Jovymar, the eldest, had started to cut sugarcane for 100 pesos a day — hard labour for very little return.

Hers was one of the most fragile and vulnerable families and needed constant care. As a team, we gently drew her out on her skills, experience and commitment to start afresh, to succeed in a new livelihood. Broken as she was, this unimagined lifeline stirred something deep in her, and she started to come alive again. We monitored her daily at first, then weekly as her strength grew.

'When Linda arrived one day,' Mary Ann would later recall, 'I was so surprised to see anyone and wondered how they had found us in such a remote place. I was overjoyed to learn they were there to help. They gave me groceries and asked me if I had any ideas for a livelihood for myself, one that I could manage from home. At first, I could hardly believe that this was happening to me and was a little shy to put forward my ideas. Eventually, Linda and her team encouraged me to speak and I said I would like some seeds to start a market garden and some farm animals as an additional source of income.'

We began mentoring her. It was obvious that she was determined to support her family and convinced she could make her dream of a new business, a new life, a success. In a few months Mary Ann had created a large garden bursting with fruit and vegetables including eggplants, beans, tomatoes and gourds. She now sells the excess produce in the village, and the steady income means the children are back in school. When I found her working in the garden, her baby strapped on her back, she was scarcely recognisable as the same woman I had met only a few months earlier. Head held high, she looked confident and unafraid, a faint smile on her face.

The smallholding next to her modest home is alive with the sounds of the pigs and ducks that provide further income for the family.

While we recorded Mary Ann's progress, her eldest son shared his passionately held dreams on camera. Jovymar wanted to study criminology and become a police officer. His father had dreamed his son might one day attend college, the first in the family to do so. At first Jovymar believed this dream had died with his father, but he clung to his passion and purpose, and against the odds he returned to high school and worked hard each day, soaking up knowledge like a sponge. 'I want to achieve the dream of my parents and do what they were unable to do — to finish my studies and fulfil my purpose.'

As a result of the economic uplift given to Mary Ann, he was able to enrol in a four-year course in Iloilo City. He graduates as a fully trained police officer in March 2019. His additional college costs were sponsored by two amazing New Zealanders involved in Be the Change work. Jovymar is driven not just to fulfil his father's greatest wish but also to provide further support for his mother and siblings.

While 80 per cent of my work focuses on economic uplift, it always recognises the importance of playfulness. Activities that raise the spirit and get people laughing can heal the heart and soul of a community. As part of the village's psychological recovery and playfulness program, we arranged for a clown to visit. This artist was used to working in upmarket hotels in the capital and had to quickly adapt his style to a young, rural audience gathered outdoors. Nobody in Carles had seen magic before and the whole village appeared! It was truly magical to see the joy and amazement on the faces of everyone there.

I stayed in Carles for two years, during which time the fishing fleet was rebuilt and 200 families launched new small businesses with our support, from pig cooperatives to tailoring. We set up basketball and volleyball leagues on a newly built court that became a natural meeting place, drawing visitors from nearby islands and encouraging further new businesses to spring up. The newly formed basketball team needed a name, and to my surprise and delight they honoured me by choosing 'Team Cruse'. A proud moment.

Passion, purpose and playfulness.

I am currently assisting with earthquake recovery in Nepal, where I regularly get the chance to talk with a good friend, a monk from Kopan Monastery, Lama Pasang. During our last conversation, he shared with me, with his signature beaming smile, 'Our only goal in life should be happiness. Happiness for others and happiness for ourselves. Focus on kindness, altruism and service, then everything falls into place.'

We come into the world with nothing and we go with nothing. Shrouds have no pockets. However big our bank balance, we cannot take it with us. There is no prize at the end of life for what we have accumulated. When we start to live with happiness as our goal we automatically connect with our passion and purpose. There is no public path. Each of us has our own talents and gifts. Happiness comes when we use them.

Live with no regrets. Follow your dream, not someone else's…

See you on the frontline.

Linda

Nepal, July 2018

LINDA CRUSE

Thank you for reading
Leading on the Frontline.

To continue your leadership journey
and to access free learning and
leadership resources visit:

www.leadingonthefrontline.com

LINDA  CRUSE

To find out more about Linda's work visit:

Website: www.lindacruse.com
www.therace4good.com

YouTube: www.youtube.com/channel/UCkIVsfjgWimca6vjp
GHAG3A/videos

Facebook: www.facebook.com/BeTheChangeProgramme

Twitter: www.twitter.com/BTCfrontline

LinkedIn: www.linkedin.com/in/lindacruse

Index